NORTH AMERICA'S
GREAT RAILROADS

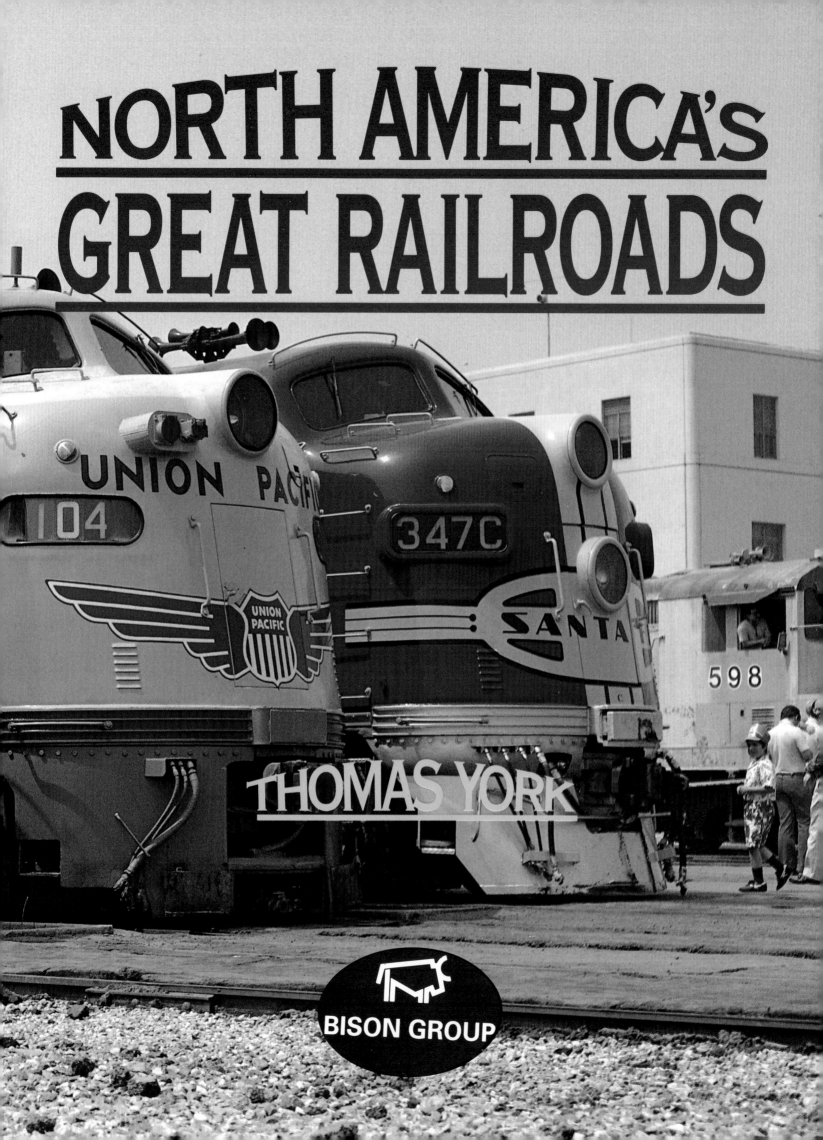

NORTH AMERICA'S
GREAT RAILROADS

THOMAS YORK

BISON GROUP

First Published in 1987 by
Bison Books Ltd
Kimbolton House
117A Fulham Road
London SW3 6RL
England

ISBN 0 86124 372 2

Printed in Hong Kong

Reprinted 1991

Designed by Ruth DeJauregui

Edited by Timothy Jacobs, John Kirk,
 and Frank Lowney

Acknowledgements

We would like to thank the railroad companies
without whose generous assistance this book
would not have been possible.

Photo Credits

All photos were provided by the railroad companies except:
© American Graphic Systems Archives: 41(bottom), 49 (top), 60–
 61, 64 (top), 65, 68 (left), 80, 91, 92 (left), 97, 112 (bottom), 125
 (top and bottom), 142, 153 (top), 183
Baltimore & Ohio Railroad Museum: 4–5, 163 (bottom),
 164 (bottom), 165, 166
Baltimore & Ohio Railroad Company: 7
Bancroft Library, University of California Berkeley: 13 (right),
 14 (bottom), 51, 76–77 (bottom), 78 (left)

Bison Picture Library: 6, 33, (top), 116–117 (bottom), 181 (bottom)
Orville Brent: 101 (bottom)
H L Broadbelt Collection: 163 (top), 171, 184 (bottom)
Tom Brown: 10
CSX Corporation: 1
California State Railroad Museum: 186 (bottom)
Canadian National Rail: 2–3, 9 (top)
Canadian Pacific Rail: 190
The Library of Congress Collections: 20 (top)
John B Corns: 160, 161 (bottom), 168, 172–173, 174 (left and right)
George W Hamlin: 167 (top), 169 (left and top right), 176, 188 (bot-
 tom)
Mid-Continent Railway Museum: 118 (bottom left)
National Railway Historical Society: 19 (top), 20 (bottom), 58–59
 (bottom), 108 (bottom)
New York Central Historical Society: 178, 179 (top and bottom), 182
 (top and bottom)
New York Public Library Picture Collection: 45 (bottom), 60 (left)
Santa Fe Southern Pacific Corporation: 8, 9 (bottom), 191
Union Pacific Historical Collection: 44 (bottom)
Union Pacific Railroad Museum Collection: 42, 46–47, 49 (bottom),
 50, 52 (top and middle), 54–55, 56–57 (left), 62 (top)
© Bill Yenne: 101 (top), 105 (bottom), 177 (bottom)

Page 1: In a scene from the 1950s, a Seaboard
Lines engineer returns—with hand, whistle, bell
and airhorn—the salute of a boy, his dog, and
history. *Pages 2–3:* A Canadian National diesel
hauls a coal train through the beautiful and
rugged Alberta countryside. *These pages:* The
B&O Railroad Depot at Harper's Ferry, West Virginia, as photographed on 13 August 1931.

CONTENTS

INTRODUCTION

The Beginnings

The history of North America is mirrored in the history of railroads in the United States and Canada during the 19th and 20th centuries. Before the invention of the steam engine, the first so-called 'railroads' were primitive affairs—wooden-railed tramways with carts and wagons pulled by mules, horses or oxen.

The distinction of operating the first tramway goes to Canada, where it was used to haul commercial goods and military supplies up and over the Niagara escarpment near the New York state border in 1762. Other tram systems were later constructed in Pennsylvania and Massachusetts as the device became popular.

Before long, the trains—nothing more than carriages with wheels mounted on wooden rails and pulled by horses—were constructed in many communities on the eastern seaboard. Then in the 1820s, Thomas Watt's steam engine, which had ushered in the Industrial Revolution in Europe, arrived in the form of the steam locomotive.

The inventors on this continent followed the lead established in England by Robert Stephenson, who built the first steam locomotives in the 1820s and shipped them to the New World. One of his first, *The Stourbridge Lion,* was shipped to the Delaware and Hudson Railway. Then the financiers and builders actually put the new invention to work and expanded a network of rails.

Stephenson's locomotive stirred the imaginations of many American and Canadian inventors. Peter Cooper, a Baltimore merchant, for example, designed and constructed the first North American locomotive, the *Tom Thumb,* in the 1830s with an upright boiler and steam tubes made from gun barrels. Others, like Ross Winans, followed in his footsteps.

Within a few years, the Baltimore & Ohio held a contest to challenge the ingenuity of the best inventors of the era. The result was a locomotive that could pull 15 tons of gross weight at 15 miles per hour. After the introduction of those first home-made machines, US railroads never looked back, and within a decade, thousands of miles of track were under construction. Americans and Canadians abandoned the horse and buggy—and the canal barge—for the speed and efficiency of the steam locomotive, just as ancient man had embraced the wheel.

Opposite: **An early wood burner pulls up to the water tank. HD Stitt's depiction of the *Tom Thumb's* race against horse power is shown *below.***

It took a few years to get momentum going, but soon the continent was humming with the clanking, banging and hissing of steam engines. The network of wood and steel exploded, and trains began running from town to town, city to city and state to state. Some of the early railroads chartered in those heady early days of the first steam locomotives—such as the Chesapeake & Ohio, the Baltimore & Ohio, the New York Central and the Pennsylvania—survived for more than 130 years.

Wherever citizens needed quick, reliable transportation, railroads sprang up like weeds after a summer rain. From 1840 to 1850 the number of rail miles grew from 2500 to 9000, and by 1860—on the eve of the Civil War—the number of miles had trebled.

The war held up construction of many new railroads—although the steam locomotive proved to be a decisive factor in the Union's victory over the South. But after the fighting, especially in the western provinces and territories of Canada and in the region west of the Mississippi in the US, government land grants and subsidies generated a great boom in rail construction. At that time some of the greatest railroad companies in the history of transportation were created—such names as the Southern Pacific, the Union Pacific, the Northern Pacific, the Canadian Pacific, the Great Northern and the Santa Fe.

Growth did not come without problems, however, and all railroads fell prey to accidents and wrecks and the resulting horrors of death and injury. Even economic and political crises on a national level were created by such so-called 'robber barons' of the day as Daniel Drew, Jim Fisk, Jay Gould and Cornelius Vanderbilt. These men and others like them were accused of having schemed, fought and plotted and then plundered the assets of the fledgling American railroads. Yet just when they seemed to be riding high the times abruptly changed and the railroads were released from the tyranny of back-room deals, stock manipulations and powerful corporate trusts.

During World War I, when railroad managers were unable to coordinate the orderly transportation of men and materials to Atlantic coast ports for shipment to Europe, the US government took over the railroads and railroad mileage reached record levels. After the war, the government returned the railroads to private enterprise, but by that time a steady decline had begun in the total number of miles of track in use each year.

In the prosperity of the 1920s, the personal automobile and the truck began making inroads on passenger and freight traffic, and when the Depression struck, many railroads were deeply in debt for lack of revenue and fell into bankruptcy.

The switch from steam to diesel began in the 1930s, although the changeover slowed during World War II. But at the end of the fighting the pace of change accelerated, and by the end of the 1950s, steam locomotives had all but disappeared from North American railroads.

In the age of merger and acquisition in the 1960s and 1970s, many of the venerable names and corporate logos disappeared—names like the Wabash, the Nickel Plate, the Chesapeake & Ohio and the Atlantic Coast Line, as well as the New York Central, the Pennsylvania and the Chicago, Burlington & Quincy. In Canada, the Canadian National is the result of the merger and consolidation of 221 railroads that began during the 19th century.

This is the story of eight great North American railroads, those that survived the rough and tumble of more than 150 years of railroad history. They include the Canadian Pacific, the Canadian National, the Southern Pacific, the Union Pacific, and the Atchison, Topeka & Santa Fe, all of whom are grand old names of the Golden Age of American railroading.

Among them are newer names that represent the heritage of other grand old names from the 'Golden Age.' These are the CSX Corp (incorporating the Baltimore & Ohio, the Chessie System and the Seaboard), the Burlington Northern (incorporating the Great Northern, the Northern Pacific and the Chicago, Burlington & Quincy) and finally Conrail (incorporating the Pennsylvania and the New York Central).

This is also the story of the men who built these great empires, who helped industrialize the continent and settle the west in both the United States and Canada. It describes the struggle to survive against the winds of economic change during the 19th and 20th centuries. These eight railroads were selected because they represent the best of hundreds of railroads that once flourished.

To begin, we will trace the history of one of the greatest engineering feats of that age: the building of the transcontinental railroad across the mountains, deserts and plains of the great American west. We will continue with accounts of the great eastern railroads, the pioneering railroads of the Pacific northwest, and the two continental Canadian railroads.

Below left: Atchison, Topeka & Santa Fe steam versus stagecoach was no contest—the AT&SF embodied speed, comfort and Fred Harvey's good food. The hauling power of railroads today: *at right,* a Canadian National diesel leads dozens of tank cars; *below:* a seemingly endless Southern Pacific coal train.

SOUTHERN PACIFIC

The Southern Pacific

The story of the Southern Pacific is a story of guts and determination. It is the story of four Sacramento merchants who created a major transportation empire after the golden spike had been driven into the last tie at Promontory, Utah.

These four men—Collis P Huntington, Leland Stanford, Charles Crocker and Mark Hopkins—parlayed the great risks of building a railroad into immense individual fortunes. Unlike the financial speculators, who drove so many early railroads to bankruptcy and ruin, these men shaped their railroad into a shipping and transportation empire that has endured for more than 125 years.

Today the Southern Pacific Transportation Company—an independent trust of the Chicago-based Santa Fe Southern Pacific Corporation—is one of the largest railroads in the United States. As of December 1985, the Southern Pacific (SP) operated trains over more than 13,500 miles of track, which extends from Oregon to California, through Nevada, Utah, Arizona, New Mexico, Texas and Louisiana and north to Kansas, Missouri and Tennessee.

In the mid-1980s, the Southern Pacific owned or leased nearly 2500 locomotives and nearly 60,000 freight cars, carrying everything from grain, chemicals and coal to lumber and wood products.

The Southern Pacific today is a railroad in transition, struggling to survive increasing competitive pressures—not only from the trucking and airline industries, but from other rail carriers as well. In the coming years, as a consequence, the SP expects to sell or abandon approximately 3100 miles of mainline and branch track and dispose of nearly 10,000 freight cars and 400 locomotives. The cutbacks will result in the loss of 3800 employees.

Eventually, Santa Fe Southern Pacific will merge the Southern Pacific with the Atchison, Topeka & Santa Fe Railroad. When that day comes, the story of one of the great American railroads will end, a story impossible to separate from the saga of America's westward migration in the 19th and early 20th centuries.

As one company brochure proclaimed, 'SP helped develop the west, and the west in turn helped develop SP. SP's history is, in fact, impossible to separate from the pageant of American's westward migration in the 19th and 20th centuries.'

Opposite: **A Southern Pacific diesel hauls pickup trucks and other freight through Guadalupe, California.** *Below:* **A triple-header SP freight train.**

The 'Pacific Railroad'

As America's fledgling railroad network expanded east of the Mississippi, the promise of a transcontinental line took shape.After the discovery of gold in 1848 at Sutter's Mill, a national rail link with California took on great urgency. Between 1850 and 1860 the number of rail miles more than tripled as the railroad gained in popularity for both moving freight and carrying passengers. Several people stepped forward to advance the concept of a 'Pacific railroad,' but it took nearly two decades to get the project financed and rolling. As the years passed, the US government took greater interest in building a transcontinental railroad and ordered several studies to determine the best route to California.

The Golden State, which had been admitted to the Union in 1850 after the great Gold Rush of 1849, was more than 2000 miles from the closest railroad on the Mississippi and was separated from the rest of the Union by a wide expanse of prairie, deserts and craggy, snow-capped mountains. Those who ventured west by ship travelled for more than 15,000 miles around the tip of South America or risked malaria and other tropical diseases by taking a shortcut across Panama. Those venturing west by foot, horse or wagon train spent six months on rugged trails, vulnerable not only to nature but also to Indian attacks. Furthermore, the increasing trade between San Francisco and major banking centers like New York City, Boston and Baltimore was hindered by the great distance.

Californians wanted a transcontinental railroad, but they knew it would require a line two and one-half times as long as any that had been built—a monumental task that discouraged most people from tackling it.

One man who thought it could be done was Theodore D Judah, who was not deterred by the distance or the obstacles. He believed the great mountain passes of the Sierra Nevadas and Rockies could be crossed with railroad tracks. Judah, like many other Californians, argued that the federal government owed the state a railroad in exchange for the gold and taxes that were shipped east. Some citizens even threatened to pull out of the Union if a railroad was not built, and their threats grew louder with the approach of the Civil War.

Judah was 28 years old when he arrived in California in 1854 to survey and build the state's first rail system—the Sacramento Valley Railroad (now one of the oldest segments of the Southern Pacific system). The Sacramento Valley was a short line, running 23 miles from Sacramento to Folsom, but it served miners and others who traveled to and from the fabled Mother Lode in the foothills east of Sacramento.

Judah had something bigger in mind than surveying a short line to the gold fields. He wanted to bridge the Sierra Nevadas with a railroad, then push it east to the Mississippi River. 'It will be built, and I will have something to do with it,' he told his wife.

By the late 1850s, Judah had scouted the granite canyons of the Sierras and completed preliminary surveys of possible routes. All he needed was the capital with which to get it started. He first attempted to sell financiers in San Francisco on the idea, but they turned him down. He then led the Pacific Railroad Convention, held in San Francisco in 1859, to generate interest in his project and undertook many private trips to Washington, DC to lobby members of Congress.

Possessed by his vision, Judah stopped all those who would listen. However, businessmen in San Francisco, who depended

on shipping for their business, rejected his arguments. They did not share Judah's conviction that a transcontinental railroad could be built.

Above: Leland Stanford, the first president of the Central Pacific. *Above left:* Collis P Huntington, the first vice president of the Central Pacific. *Above opposite:* Theodore D Judah, the visionary who inspired the Central Pacific. *Below opposite:* California's first locomotive, the 4–4–0 *Sacramento.*

The Big Four

Judah returned to Sacramento discouraged but still determined, and continued to seek out men willing to finance his scheme. by holding private meetings and conferences he came across the four Sacramento merchants who were to shape the destiny of the American west. The four—Collis P Huntington, Leland Stanford, Mark Hopkins, and Charles Crocker—were to go down in history as 'The Big Four.'

No simple visionary, Judah was astute enough to know that these merchants would not consider just any railroad proposal. He had to promise them a project that could be built inexpensively, on modest investments, yet earn large returns.

By building a railroad through the Sierras, he explained, the merchants could monopolize trade with silver-rich western Nevada and cities like Carson City and Virginia City. The merchants knew the expense involved in carrying goods to eastern Nevada via the existing muddy, rocky wagon roads. They regularly shipped equipment, supplies and food by wagons and horses across the Sierras, but the trip was treacherous, time-consuming and costly. Judah said a railroad could do it quickly and they all would make fortunes in the process.

Huntington listened to Judah, then took the idea to his fellow storekeepers. When Huntington and the others decided that it was not only feasible, but highly profitable, they set down to plan their railroad. It was unusual to find four such visionary men who got along with each other—unlike railroad

moguls and barons in the east who fought constantly, refusing to cooperate or work together. The Big Four were middle-class, hard-working mature men who wanted to achieve a common goal.

By the time the project got under way in the early 1860s, Huntington was a hardware dealer in his late 30s. He quickly emerged as the leader, assuming the role of capitalist by raising funds for the undertaking. Huntington would later spend much of his time in the east to keep the project financed.

Having been on his own since age 13, Huntington knew how to drive a bargain. He had ventured to California from a Connecticut farm where he had saved every penny of his $7 monthly salary. En route, he sold jewelry, butter and several kegs of whiskey (making a handsome profit on the whiskey). He left the east with $1200 in his pocket; when he reached California he had $5000. A shrewd, savvy man, he worked with little sleep or relaxation. He became the pivotal character behind the success of both the transcontinental railroad and the early Southern Pacific Transportation Company.

Leland Stanford, one of the three New Yorkers in the group, was the son of a post-road innkeeper who had earned a small fortune during the Gold Rush. Stanford was the most prosperous of the four. He had studied law, but made his money in the grocery business in Sacramento.

Stanford was the politician of the group, having been a delegate to the 1860 Republican convention in Chicago where Abraham Lincoln was nominated for president. He had become governor of California by the time the transcontinental

14

Charles Crocker, shown *above* surrounded by his family, was construction supervisor for the CP. Mark Hopkins *(below left)* handled the accounting chores for the railroad and kept his partners working with—as opposed to against—one another. *Right:* A pre-1870 photo of the CP's Sacramento yard.

project got under way and was later elected to the US Senate. Despite his political successes, Stanford was notorious for windy speeches and a dull intellect.

Mark Hopkins—Huntington's partner in the hardware business and known for his integrity and honesty—kept the books and the paperwork for the project. Hopkins was frugal but friendly and was responsible for keeping his partners working harmoniously when they fought. He was the oldest of the quartet: age 49 when the project was organized in 1861.

Charles Crocker, a rotund, burly, dry goods merchant (weighing more than 250 pounds), took command of the physical task of building the railroad. Originally from New York where he had been a farm hand, sawmill helper and blacksmith, Crocker came to California during the Gold Rush, then drove freight wagons in the gold fields.

The Central Pacific Railroad Company of California was incorporated on 28 June 1861, with Stanford as president, Huntington as vice president, Hopkins as treasurer and Judah as chief engineer. The four set the original stock offering at 85,000 shares with a par value of $100 per share. They had hoped to sell most shares in San Francisco, but raised only $1500.

San Franciscans showed little interest in a project directed by four Sacramento shopkeepers. Behind the scenes, many believed that if the project were successful, it would threaten the local economy which depended heavily on shipping.

Undaunted by poor stock sales, the Big Four decided to build the railroad anyway, pledging their personal fortunes and credit and then lobbying the California state legislature for financial support. Prodded by Stanford, who by then was governor, the lawmakers passed several bills authorizing San

Francisco, Sacramento and Placer counties to buy CP stock. San Francisco was later allowed to donate $600,000 in lieu of a stock purchase.

Theodore Judah meanwhile went to Washington to enlist the help of the federal government. By the summer of 1862, his vision of a transcontinental railroad was shared by a majority in Congress. Civil War had erupted, and President Lincoln had decided that a railroad was needed to draw California closer to the Union. Congress agreed and passed the Pacific Railroad Act, which authorized the Central Pacific—(the CP) later part of the Southern Pacific system—to build east from Sacramento while the Union Pacific (the UP) would drive west from the Missouri River.

When the legislation was signed, it was a day of great celebration because government support ensured that they had the necessary financial backing to undertake a Pacific railroad. Judah sent a telegram to his Sacramento partners: 'We have drawn the elephant,' he wrote.'Now let us see if we can harness him up.'

Congress agreed to contribute lands and proceeds from the sale of bonds to help spur construction. Both companies were given a 400-foot right-of-way across government lands, which they needed for stations, switch yards and shops. They were also granted 10 sections of land—later increased to 20—for each mile completed. The proceeds from the sale of 30-year US bonds were loaned to the railroads in varying amounts depending on the difficulty of construction at various points during the job.

The act called for interest payments of six percent by the two companies. Huntington was able to convince officials to delay interest payments until the bonds matured. Later, however, he refused to repay the bonds until forced to do so by federal authorities.

Although the incentives were generous, they proved insufficient for a project of such scope. The CP was given two years to build the first 50 miles to qualify for subsidies. Then it was required to build 50 miles per year until the California-Nevada border was crossed. For the Big Four, it was a struggle to build even the first 50 miles. For example, three years passed before the UP was able to lay the first rails west of Omaha, Nebraska.

The slow start so concerned Lincoln and the Congress that in 1864 and again in 1866 the lawmakers repealed legislation forbidding the Central Pacific from building more than 150 miles east of the California-Nevada border. Since land was granted on the amount of trackage completed, the undertaking, deemed so difficult in earlier years, suddenly became a great public contest between the CP and the UP to see who could build the most track. By the time construction crews from both railroads got up to speed after the end of the Civil War, the project commanded the imagination of the nation.

Construction Begins

After the passage of the Pacific Railroad Act, Judah returned to California, completed his working surveys, and picked the Donner Summit as the best route for the railroad. Meanwhile, Huntington went east to buy supplies and equipment, carrying documents from his three associates that gave him unlimited powers of attorney.

When he found credit unavailable, Huntington telegraphed for personally-signed blank checks on the personal accounts of his partners, which guaranteed the government bonds he was trying to sell. While risky—the men stood to lose their entire personal fortunes—his actions ensured that the work in California would continue.

Ground was broken in January 1863 with great ceremony. But actual construction did not get under way until October when the first rails were laid in Sacramento. Huntington, however, remained in the east, not even bothering to return to attend. He even wrote a letter saying he opposed the celebration. 'If you want to jubilate in driving the first spike, go ahead and do it. I don't,' he wrote. 'Those mountains look too ugly and I see too much work ahead.'

The first CP locomotive arrived 10 months later when *The Governor Stanford* was unloaded at dockside in Sacramento, but it was nearly lost before it could be put to work: the longshoremen almost dropped it into the cold waters of the Sacramento River as it was being hoisted off the ship.

Next came *The Pacific* and then Central Pacific No 3, *The CP Huntington*, which was later numbered as Southern Pacific No 1. This locomotive was typical of American locomotives of the era. It was almost 30 feet long, and builders said that it could haul four cars weighing 22 tons each at 35 miles per hour, up a grade of 26 feet per mile. (But train engineers never achieved that goal.) Later, Engine No 4 arrived and was named *The TD Judah* in honor of CP's chief engineer.

Two major problems confronted the CP in the early years: material shortages caused by the Civil War and labor shortages. For example, the Pacific Railroad Act had required the railroads to buy rails forged in the United States. But with domestic mills committed to turning out war materials, rail prices doubled and became a costly requirement for the CP.

The war also increased shipping costs to California. The first locomotive shipped 'round the Horn' cost the Central Pacific $2282 in freight charges. Later the cost rose to $8100 to ship a similar size locomotive. But the charges had to be paid or else no work could be done.

Labor shortages proved a bigger drawback than material shortages. In the early days, the men whom Crocker hired did not remain at work for long. They soon abandoned their picks and shovels for the gold mines of the Mother Lode and western Nevada. Crocker estimated that he lost 1900 of the 2000 men he had hired in one short period of time.

In desperation, he turned to Chinese laborers, many of whom had been brought to California to work the gold mines. They wanted work and were known to be industrious and diligent, so Crocker tested 50 men on a portion of the project. They proved their skill so well that soon thousands of Chinese were brought from Hong Kong and southern China and put to work digging and blasting.

Although paid almost as much as the Caucasians, they were far more productive. By the time the railroad was completed, more than 12,000 Chinese were on the CP payroll. In addition to their ability with picks and shovels, the Chinese were experts in explosives like black powder and nitroglycerin—both used to blast the grey and white granite of the Sierras.

The Chinese were disparagingly called 'Crocker's pets,' and were hardly mentioned during the historic connection ceremonies at Promontory, Utah. For many years afterward, their work went unrecognized except for a few sentences in history books. But the Chinese, laboring long hours under harsh conditions without complaint—much of their work completed without machinery or equipment—deserve most of the credit for building the main line of the CP from Sacramento to Promontory.

Crocker did as much as he could to keep the Asians satisfied and working. They were fed such familiar foods from the Orient, as for example, dried oysters, cuttlefish, seaweed, bamboo shoots as well as sweet rice crackers, desiccated vegetables, rice, pork and poultry. On the job they drank hot tea drawn from whiskey barrels.

The Chinese were sometimes taunted and teased by the Irish work gangs, though, especially when they met up with their counterparts from the Union Pacific. But they refused to be intimidated and went to great lengths to take care of their own. When—as a 'practical' joke by Union Pacific workmen—several Asian workers were blown up with black powder, the Chinese retaliated by first mining the ground underneath a Union Pacific work crew and then setting off the charge. Several men were buried under a cascade of broken rock and dirt.

By 1867, CP crews had blasted and dug their way through the imposing Sierra Nevadas. To do so, 15 tunnels had to be bored through granite and other hard rock, and 40 miles of wooden snow sheds had to be constructed. To penetrate and blast the rock, the Chinese used black powder—then the more powerful nitroglycerin. The work was agonizingly slow, while snow and cold often kept the men from working during the winter months. So to make up for lost time, three shifts labored around the clock in the summer.

One great achievement was construction of the snow sheds used to protect trains and crews from winter snow storms. To protect mountain tracks from deep snow and avalanches, the

Opposite: **The Central Pacific's Number 3, aka the *CP Huntington,* helped with the building of the transcontinental railroad. *Above:* A tea carrier bringing refreshment to his fellow Chinese track workers—who are visible in the photo *below* of the Secrettown Trestle, in the Sierra Nevadas, circa 1867.**

superintendent of building and bridges came up with the idea to build sheds. 'Let's build a roof over the railroad,' he suggested.

Tested in 1867, the sheds proved so successful in keeping out the snow that winter that 25 carpenters were put to work building more sheds. So much wood was required that when the mills ran out of timber the men had to stop work and venture into the nearby forests to cut their own wood. Eventually, more than 65 million board feet of timber was used to cover 40 miles of track in California's high country to protect the trains from snow (though the view from passing passenger trains was cut off).

By 1868, CP gangs were racing eastward across the Nevada and Utah deserts at the rate of more than a mile a day. Union Pacific gangs, meanwhile, were racing westward. When CP construction boss Charles Crocker heard that the UP crews had beaten the previous record of eight miles in one day, he bet $10,000 that his crews could do better. They did—on 28 April 1869.

That day the Chinese workmen moved out at dawn, armed with a carefully prepared game plan. By the end of the day, they had constructed 10 miles and 12 feet of track in less than 12 hours. It was an impressive feat,even winning bouquets of praise from the UP crews and track managers. It still stands as a record today when machinery is used to lay tracks.

Unlike the Union Pacific, which sometimes had trouble with marauding bands of renegade Indians, the CP had little trouble. Huntington made sure of that by giving railroad passes—good for the passenger cars—to chiefs of militant tribes, while common tribesmen and women were allowed to ride on the freight cars 'whenever they saw fit.'

In the spring of 1869, construction overlapped while the owners of the two railroads argued about where to join the last

Opposite: It was often as hard keeping the line open through the Sierran winter as it was building it. *Above:* This sign commemorates the record-setting feat of a team of workmen during the building of the transcontinental railroad. *Below:* Irish and Chinese track gangs in Nevada in 1868.

rails of the transcontinental railroad. The site they agreed upon was located in the middle of Utah Territory at Promontory, north of the Great Salt Lake. It was 690 miles from Sacramento and 1086 miles from Omaha.

On 10 May, two locomotives—the CP's *Jupiter* and Union Pacific's No 119—chugged up to each other to signal completion of the ambitious project. Speeches and photography marked the ceremonies.

No one knows for sure, but it is believed that it cost the Central Pacific more than $27 million to build its 1171 miles of track. The Big Four had risked hundred of thousands of dollars from their own pocketbooks, but now they possessed the proceeds from the sale of $25 million in government bonds and held title to 4.5 million acres of former public lands.

At top, above: A CP line camp in Utah in April of 1869. *At left:* The CP's *Jupiter* during the golden spike ceremonies on 10 May 1869. *Below:* The *Jupiter* greets the last wagon train to cross the prairie. *Opposite:* Amos Bowsher recalls for his friends the joining of east and west.

PACIFIC RAILROAD.

Time Table No. 6.   To take effect Feb. 14, 1865.

TRAINS GOING EAST.					TRAINS GOING WEST	
Freight. No. 3.	Mail & Pass., No. 1.	Distance fr. Sac.	STATIONS.	Dist. fr. N.	Mail & Pass, No. 2.	Freight. No. 4.
2 P.M.. Dp..........	6.30 A.M. Dp.........		Sacramento..	31...	11.50 A.M. Arr.....	7.25 P M. Arr.........
2.35	6.55	7 ..	Arcade.........	24 ..	11.25	6 55 ....
3.00	7.10 ...._	15...	Antelope	16...	11.10	6.30 ....
3.25	7.20	18...	Junction ...	13...	11 00	6.15 ....
3.45	7.30	22...	Rocklin ...	9...	10.45	5.50 ....
4.05	7.40	25...	Pino	6...	10.35	5 32 ....
4.40 P. M. Arr......	8.00 A M Arr.........	31...	Newcastle ...		10.15 A.M. Dp.....	5.00 P.M. Dp ....

No Trains will leave any Station ahead of time, unless specially ordered by Superintendent.

Gravel and Extra Trains must keep ten minutes out of the way of all regular Trains.

NIGHT SIGNALS.—A light swung over the head is a signal to go ahead.

When swung across, or at right angles with the track, is a signal to back up, and when moved up and down, is a signal to stop.

C. CROCKER, Superintendent.

ANNUAL - - - 1869.

Central Pacific
RAILROAD.

PASS J. J. Orr

in this State —

Subject to the Conditions printed on the back of this Pass, until

Dec 31 1869,

unless otherwise ordered.

E. B. Crocker

Gen'l Supt.

May 31 1869. No.

Above: The first official timetable for the Central Pacific, published when the line was opened from Sacramento to Newcastle on 6 June 1864. *At left and below:* Various passes used on the CP, including *immediately below,* passes issued to Jennie Stanford. *Below right:* An interior view of a passenger coach, circa 1870; the seats shown here are of more recent design.

CENTRAL PACIFIC RAILROAD CO.
AND LEASED LINES.

No. 23.—

Special Ticket for the use of

1882

Miss Jennie Stanford.

Acct of Complimentary.

To be void after

June 30,

1882.

Leland Stanford

SUBJECT TO CONDITIONS ON REVERSE SIDE.

A

CENTRAL PACIFIC R. R. CO.
and Leased Lines.

This ticket is issued by the above named Company, and accepted by the person herein named, on the conditions hereinafter set forth :

The person who accepts this ticket thereby assumes all risk of accidents, and in consideration of its receipt expressly agrees that the above Company shall not be liable, under any circumstances, whether by negligence, criminal or otherwise—of its agents or others, for any injury to the person, or for loss or injury to property, while using this ticket, and that as to such person the above Company shall not be considered as common carriers, or liable as such.

This ticket IS NOT TRANSFERABLE, and if presented by any other person than the party issued for, the Conductor will take it up and collect FULL TRAIN RATES.

I hereby agree that this ticket is subject to the above conditions, and that I will make my signature whenever required by the Company's Agents or Conductors.

Expires Dec. 31st,
1882,
Unless limited to
a prior date.

The party for whom this ticket is issued must sign his signature [in the blank] in ink, before presenting it for passage. Conductors will not recognize this ticket unless signed.

(Sign in Ink—do not use Pencil.)

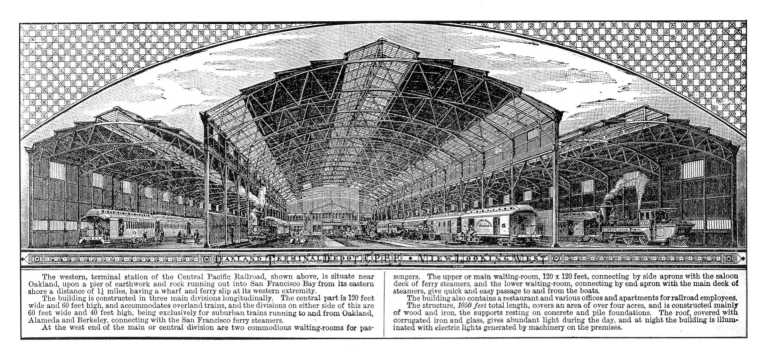

The western, terminal station of the Central Pacific Railroad, shown above, is situate near Oakland, upon a pier of earthwork and rock running out into San Francisco Bay from its eastern shore a distance of 1¼ miles, having a wharf and ferry slip at its western extremity.

The building is constructed in three main divisions longitudinally. The central part is 120 feet wide and 60 feet high, and accommodates overland trains, and the divisions on either side of this are 60 feet wide and 40 feet high, being exclusively for suburban trains running to and from Oakland, Alameda and Berkeley, connecting with the San Francisco ferry steamers.

At the west end of the main or central division are two commodious waiting-rooms for pas-

sengers. The upper or main waiting-room, 120 x 120 feet, connecting by side aprons with the saloon deck of ferry steamers, and the lower waiting-room, connecting by end apron with the main deck of steamers, give quick and easy passage to and from the boats.

The building also contains a restaurant and various offices and apartments for railroad employees.

The structure, *1050 feet* total length, covers an area of over four acres, and is constructed mainly of wood and iron, the supports resting on concrete and pile foundations. The roof, covered with corrugated iron and glass, gives abundant light during the day, and at night the building is illuminated with electric lights generated by machinery on the premises.

Regular Passenger Service

Regular freight and passenger service began just five days after the celebration at Promontory, with one passenger train running each way—each day. Westbound it was known as *The Pacific Express* while eastbound it was known as *The Atlantic Express*. The journey took seven days, but one special train—*The Lightning Express*—completed a run from Jersey City to San Francisco in 84 hours, 17 minutes.

CP's steam locomotives, like others of the time, were slow by modern standards, chugging across the continent at a speed of just 20 miles per hour. Yet slow as travel was, it saved months of sailing around South America or risking malaria in crossing the Isthmus of Panama.

Passenger car accommodations were simple, if not sparse. CP had no agreement with George Pullman to provide sleeping cars, so CP officials named their cars 'Silver Palace Sleeping Cars,' with seats covered with red silk plush and highlighted with oil lamps and carpets. The cars were large enough to hold 46 passengers and were kept in service until an agreement was reached with George Pullman in the 1870s to use his famous sleeping cars.

When the CP ran out of operating funds near the completion of the transcontinental project, the railroad granted food concessions at many stations. Concessionaires ran the dining room and bar and sold tickets—for a profit—but the food was not very good. Sometimes it was downright awful. However, the concessionaires generated revenue for the cash-strapped railroad.

During the early years of operation, CP locomotives were easily identified by their balloon-shaped smokestacks and famous names like *The Jupiter* and *The Arctic*. Primitive even by later steam engine standards, the locomotive boilers were made of iron plates forged together with copper-plated fireboxes and flues. Engine frames and most of the other parts were made of wrought iron and, later, of steel. Many of the locomotives were constructed at CP's own shops in Sacramento.

Opposite: Southern Pacific section men at a camp in the Tehachapi Mountains in 1875. *Below:* The 4–4–0 wood burner shown here was built in 1873—in the SP's Sacramento shops, as were many SP engines. This, and the roundhouse in the background were photographed in 1891.

The Empire Expands

While securing the transcontinental route, the Big Four consolidated and expanded in other regions. When competition from an upstart railroad that ran between San Jose and San Francisco threatened their California monopoly, they moved in and took over. For example, they bought a line known as the Southern Pacific, which its organizers planned to build down the California coast to San Diego then run eastward to New Orleans.

The CP also picked up the rights to a railroad known as the Western Pacific (no relation to the railroad which later took that name), with routes running from northern California to Oregon. The railroad was valuable to the Big Four because Congress had extended it land-grant aide just as it had to the CP, and the land promised to the Western Pacific was heavily forested.

As the empire grew, the CP in 1873 moved its corporate headquarters from Sacramento to San Francisco. In 1874 it constructed track down California's central valley to

Bakersfield, then assaulted the Tehachapi Mountains and the Mojave Desert.

Portions of this route proved to be as difficult as crossing the Sierras. The CP was faced with the task of raising the track nearly 2734 feet over a 16-mile distance from the San Joaquin Valley floor to the top of the mountain pass at Caliente. To accomplish this feat, CP engineers resorted to an ingenious but simple solution. They designed and built the famed 'Tehachapi loop' that allowed trains to circle over themselves as they climbed the 2.2 percent grade. The project also required boring 18 tunnels.

In 1876, Charles Crocker drove in a golden spike near Palmdale, California, completing the San Joaquin Valley Line and linking Los Angeles with San Francisco. By 1877 the CP had extended its track to Yuma, Arizona, thereby becoming the first railroad operating in that state.

Later, CP took the rights to the route beyond Yuma and put crews to work constructing track eastward to El Paso to meet up with short-haul lines. In the process the CP picked up scores of railroads and merged them into its system. (Those

lines make up the oldest component of the modern Southern Pacific system. The original railroad dates back to 1851 when the Buffalo Bayou, Brazos & Colorado Railway was started near Houston.)

New Orleans was brought into the system when the last spike was driven near the Pecos River in 1883. This route, connecting New Orleans with Los Angeles and known as the Sunset Route, was the most famous of what became the Southern Pacific Lines.

The identity of Central Pacific disappeared in the 1880s. The Southern Pacific Companies of California and of Texas were incorporated under the laws of Kentucky in 1884. Leland Stanford was elected president of the SP, and the old name of 'Central Pacific Railroad' began to disappear from locomotives and rolling stock.

SP grew rapidly to become more than just a railroad. Steamships and ferries were added and became an integral part of its transportation system for many years. For example, until completion of a $10 million bridge across the Suisun Straits northeast of San Francisco, much SP traffic was carried to Oakland, where the cars were ferried across the Bay to San Francisco.

SP also operated a passenger ferryboat service on San Francisco Bay. The peak year of service came in 1930 when the company operated 43 boats—the world's largest fleet—carrying 40 million passengers and six million automobiles and trucks.

With completion of the San Francisco-Oakland Bay Bridge in 1936 and the Golden Gate Bridge in 1937, ferry service began to diminish, then disappear entirely. The last SP ferry ran on the San Francisco Bay in 1958, a year which happened to coincide with the last trip of an SP steam engine from San Francisco to Reno, occurring just 11 years after the first mainline diesel freight locomotives were placed in service.

Zulu Trains

In 1870 the CP began advertising nationwide and started European campaigns to attract settlers to the west. Lured by cheap land and low fares, trains filled with emigrants were soon carrying families, furniture and livestock to the California

paradise. One advertisement printed in 1875 read: 'Ho for California! The Laborer's Paradise! Salubrious Climate, Fertile Soil, Larger Labor Returns, No Severe Winters, No Lost Time, No Blight or Insect Pests!'

In 1869 the first-class fare between Chicago and San Francisco was set at $130 but was cut to $118 four years later. Second-class fare was even less—$85. When a fare war erupted between the SP and rival Santa Fe in 1886, it caused the bottom to fall out of the rate structure.

Soon, railroads offered to carry passengers from points west of Missouri to the west coast for as little as $12. Santa Fe dropped them even lower—to $6 and then $1—before jacking them back up to $40 for second-class passengers and $50 for first-class riders. When families in the east heard about the cheap fares, they eagerly joined the westward migration.

Fares for 'land seeker' tickets could be applied to railway land purchases—most of which had been granted to the railroad by the federal government. This land, which sold for as little as $1 to $10 an acre, could be purchased in installments and colonists who settled together received group rates. Bet-

Top of page: The Southern Pacific station at Beaumont, Texas. *Below: The San Gabriel* was the first locomotive in Southern California. *Above right:* Number 2127 was built at the Sacramento shops in 1888. *Below right:* This engine was decorated for President Benjamin Harrison's train from LA in 1891.

ween 1901 and 1916, more than 800,000 of these settlers took advantage of the low fares.

The SP soon operated hundreds of 'Zulu cars'—flat cars loaded with immigrants and their household goods pulled by freight trains. One member of the family rode on the Zulu car to watch the livestock and belongings, while other family members traveled in passenger cars. In one year, more than 120,000 immigrants ventured to southern California.

With so many people pouring into the state, towns and cities began to spring up overnight. In fact, 60 new towns were laid out within three years along SP tracks, while more than $200 million in real estate transactions were recorded in one year.

For the arriving settlers, the SP hired agricultural advisers to help develop new crops and irrigation methods especially suited to California conditions. Later, refrigerator cars were devised that could transport fruit and vegetables to distant markets in the east and midwest.

'Exhibit trains'—promoting western products and opportunities—were sent around the nation. Lecturers were sent to Europe to promote California sunshine, agricultural products like oranges and scenic wonders such as Yosemite and the redwoods. Much of southern California was settled on the promise of cheap land and unlimited opportunity.

SP Power

When the Big Four organized the Central Pacific, they immediately decided to have their own repair and manufacturing shops. Because the necessary equipment and materials had to be brought by ship from eastern suppliers, they could not be easily ordered and delivered. Everything needed by the CP

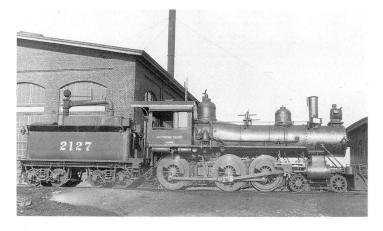

was more than 15,000 miles away, a distance that took six months to travel. So the company decided to fabricate or manufacture what it needed, itself.

Within a couple of years, shops set up at Sacramento were turning out their own rolling stock and locomotives, which worked just as well as those ordered from eastern factories, although sometimes with a few local touches.

For example, the frame of the first steam locomotive made locally was hammered from horseshoe iron that had apparently been purchased while Huntington and Hopkins were still in the hardware business. It was a 4–4–0 or American type, dubbed No 173, and was designed to burn wood, coal or sagebrush (which was especially useful when it was all that an engineer could find out in the desert.)

Most of the locomotives of the era, including those owned by CP, burned wood. Later, coal was used, and then oil at the close of the century. Oil was a favored fuel until diesel locomotives came on the scene in the 1930s. By the end of the

1950s, CP's steam locomotives had all been pulled from the system.

Most of the original locomotives on the CP roster, like *The Governor Stanford* and *The CP Huntington*, were constructed in eastern shops then shipped by sea to California. The first CP locomotive constructed specifically to haul freight was *The Connes*, or No 6, a 4–6–0 type built in Massachusetts by William Mason in 1865.

The Connes featured 17-inch diameter cylinders with a 24-inch stroke, and the driving wheels were 48 inches in diameter. With a tractive power rated at 15,350 pounds, it could haul 18 freight cars.

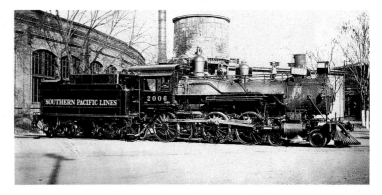

It was not long before workmen in CP's Sacramento shop developed grand ideas of their own. The size of *The Connes* was far outstripped by *El Gobernador*, the largest locomotive in the world in 1884 when it was built. It was a 4–10–0 type, designed to haul 14 30-ton cars at 10 miles an hour up the steep grades of the Tehachapi Mountains south of Bakersfield.

The engine alone weighed 146,000 pounds, with a tractive power rated at 34,500 pounds. But *El Gobernador* was too big and too heavy for regular use. Its boiler was too small to develop the power necessary to drive the locomotive and a string of freight cars. Even with two firemen aboard, *El Gobernador* could not get up enough steam. It was so large that crews feared it would tip over when rolled onto the roundhouse platform. It was finally pulled from limited service and broken up in 1894.

The Sacramento shops also turned out passenger locos, including private cars for CP executives. For example, the shops built 4–4–0s, 2–8–0s and 4–6–0s during the 1870s and 1880s. The early locomotives of the 4–6–0 type were easily identified by their massive balloon stacks, which were 54 inches in diameter and seven feet tall, designed for wood burning. When coal displaced wood, the tell-tale balloon stacks were replaced by straight stacks.

The first compound—or secondary steam cycle—locomotives of the 4–8–0 type were used on western mountain grades in the 1890s. Constructed at Schenectady, New York, they were converted to compound use at SP's shops. Other 2–8–0s purchased from New York were coal burners.

Later, SP bought 105 mogul 2–6–0 types from Schenectady and Cook at the turn of the century and used them to haul freight in California's central valley. Two years later, SP bought 18 more 4–6–0s from the Baldwin company, and later 4–4–2 Atlantic type locomotives were purchased. Although most of these were scrapped in the 1920s, four were salvaged and rebuilt and used on the *Sacramento Daylight* trains that ran in the 1940s and 1950s.

In 1902 SP, along with other western railroads, standardized locomotive designs needed for hauling freight over mountainous western terrain. The 'Associated Lines' bought locomotives with uniform designs until 1913.

Steam locomotives continued to grow in size and improve in performance throughout the 1920s and 1930s, and the SP was a leader in using advanced locomotive designs. It was among the first to purchase the 4–8–0 mountain-type locomotive built to haul trains between Los Angeles and El Paso without changing engines.

In 1930, SP adopted a standard design the 4–8–4, *General Service*- or *Golden State*-type locomotive used for both freight and passenger service. These engines pulled the famed *Daylights* of the 1930s and 1940s—like *The Shasta Daylight*

The SP loco *Umpqua* was originally Number 124, and is shown *at lower left* as Number 1212 doing service at Folsom Prison in 1900. Two convicts once hid in *Umpqua's* water tank, debarking near the town of Folsom.

SP 2006 *(above left)* is a 4–6–0 of the type turned out by the SP's Sacramento shops. *Above:* Employees of the SP's Los Angeles shops, circa 1878. *Below:* The workers at the SP's Sacramento shops in 1889.

and *The Sunset Limited*—between San Francisco and Los Angeles. Locomotives finally reached the one million pound mark with the introduction of coal-burning freight engines in New Mexico.

In the 1930s, SP introduced 'cab-in-front' steam locomotives. These were oil-fired 4–8–8–2s with the cab placed in front of the boiler and the tender trailing behind the smokebox—a design that improved visibility and threw the smoke and ash behind the train crews while they operated through the many tunnels and snow sheds in the Sierras.

By the time the Sacramento shops were shut down in 1937, more than 200 steam locomotives had been built there. With the diesel proving its value as a replacement, however, the shops were no longer needed except for repair work. The last locomotive constructed by Sacramento workmen was a switch engine.

The Octopus

While they lived, the Big Four controlled the SP with iron hands and monopolized fares and freight charges to their advantage. As a result the railroad became the most powerful economic force in California. It was a force, however, that

At left: The rear end of the SP's luxurious *Daylight* passenger train, which included a well-appointed dining car *(below)* and a spacious sleeper *(above)*.

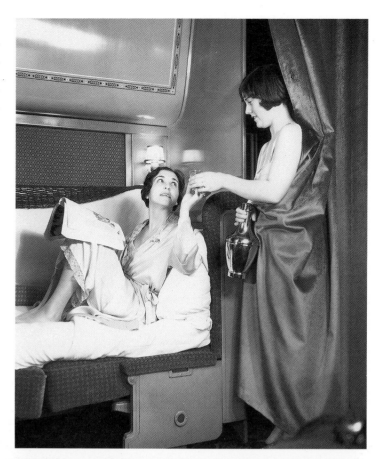

soon was resented by thousands of farmers and settlers, the same people who had been brought to California aboard the railroad. Some of these people believed that SP had reneged on its promise of giving them legal title to the land. Eventually their resentment erupted into a bloody showdown that became known as The Battle of Mussel Slough.

In 1876, some 600 settlers petitioned the government to restore to public use the land on CP's right of way between Hollister in San Benito County and Goshen in Tulare County. The settlers argued that since they had made the land valuable by farming it, they, not the SP, should be able to buy it. But the railroad, claiming title to the lands despite the fact that it had never constructed tracks along the right-of-way, began proceedings to evict the farmers.

The settlers met at Hanford in the Central Valley and organized a settlers' league after petitioning the government to retain title to the land. They offered to purchase their land at $2.50 an acre, but SP would have none of it, and the railroad's lawyers won a court order to evict the settlers. The order set up a showdown between the two sides.

When a force of men led by a federal marshal tried to move the settlers, a pitched battle erupted. Six settlers were wounded and two people representing the SP were killed. Five farmers were convicted of resisting the marshal, but they became folk heroes and when released from state prison were greeted by several thousand supporters throughout the state. The incident was later described by writer Frank Norris in his novel *The Octopus*. Norris applied the word 'octopus' to SP to symbolize the way its tentacles had reached out to control the lives of so many people.

The resentment against SP that ended in such violence along the San Joaquin Valley continued to fester throughout the west and was a principal force at the turn of the century when the Progressive Movement worked to curb the power of the railroad. In 1879, voters in California approved a railroad commission along with a new state constitution. It was not long, however before the new commission was dominated by men sympathetic to the Southern Pacific.

But the people continued to fight. Following the economic panic of 1893, reformers gathered under the banner of sugar magnate Claus Spreckels who, hoping to break the power of the Southern Pacific, led a movement to construct a railroad between Stockton and Richmond, a city on the east side of San Francisco Bay. Spreckels wanted to provide direct competition

to the Southern Pacific. The line, named the San Joaquin Valley Railroad, was later purchased by Santa Fe, which wanted entry into northern California.

Reforms in California did not end with the creation of a railroad commission. Governor Hiram Johnson took on the railroad under a campaign promise to 'kick the Southern Pacific out of politics.' He appointed new railroad commissioners and threw out those who were railroad employees. When Johnson finally smashed the old order of power established in the 1860s by the Big Four, the SP turned to the business of running a railroad and transportation company rather than running a state government.

End of an Era

The first of the Big Four entrepreneurs to pass from the scene was Mark Hopkins, who died in his sleep while on an inspection tour of the new Sunset Route of the SP. He was said to have left a fortune estimated at $50 million. Charles Crocker was the second to die—in Monterey in 1888. Leland Stanford died in 1893 in Palo Alto where he had established and endowed a private university in memory of his only son, Leland Stanford Jr. Collis Huntington was the last to die, leaving a fortune estimated in excess of $100 million.

Theodore Judah, however, the original driving force behind the success of a Pacific railroad, died in 1863 without seeing his ambition fulfilled. In that year, Judah disagreed with the headstrong Huntington and the other partners about the direction of the project and, after much argument, sold out his interest for about $100,000. He departed for New York City via the Isthmus of Panama.

Judah apparently contracted malaria or yellow fever on the trip and died shortly thereafter, his contributions never recognized by the four major partners except for their naming one of the locomotives after him. It was a paltry gesture to a man who had pushed so hard for so long to build a Pacific railroad.

After the Big Four

When Huntington died in 1900, he was one of the 35 richest men in the world. He had demonstrated skillful management during the transcontinental project, then later demonstrated his

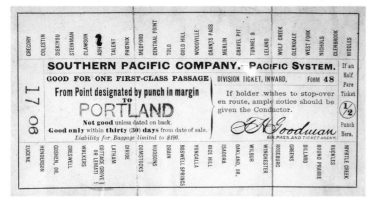

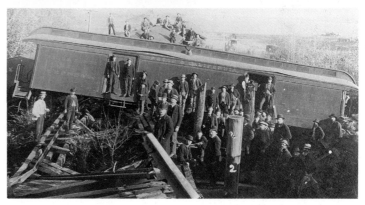

At top, above: This wreckage resulted from a collapsed trestle at Lake Labish, Oregon in 1890. *Above:* An 1898 SP ticket good from Ashland to Portland. *Above right:* A wreck on the Oregon & California line. The *Pacific Fruit Express (left)* highballs through California's Imperial Valley in 1938.

ability to compete against the best of the 'robber barons' of the east. He made many friends as well as enemies. He was firm, but could also be fair. While cold and unapproachable to outsiders, he was a warm family man to those who knew him, yet was always a special target of newspaper editorial writers and editors.

Employees knew him as an honest employer who paid well for hard work and fired on the spot those who were lazy or indolent. He held high regard for public opinion, something that his competitors in the railroad business did not always share. He once said, 'We all serve the same master, the public.'

With Huntington's death, SP leadership passed to Edward Henry Harriman, who had emerged in the public eye as a respected executive when, in 1897, he assumed control of a bankrupt Union Pacific and put it back on a sound financial footing.

Harriman, whose formal education ended when he was 14, was a shrewd Wall Street investor and speculator whose interest in railroads began with his marriage to Mary Averall, the daughter of William J Averall, president of the Ogdensburg & Lake Champlain Railroad. Harriman had purchased and rehabilitated smaller eastern railroads before becoming director of the Union Pacific in 1897.

At that time the UP had undergone hard times—it was a distressed property with deteriorating track and equipment. Harriman, however, quickly restored it to financial strength. With

Above: SP's *Overland Limited* on the Lucin Cutoff across the Great Salt Lake. *At left:* SP president EH Harriman in 1909. Pre- and post-earthquake San Francisco: The SP's station *(right)* at 3rd and Townsend, and *(below right)* SP's emergency lunchroom (EH Harriman is seated at left).

While the two railroads were under his control, the Pacific Fruit Express was jointly formed between the two companies to carry fresh fruits and vegetables across the nation in refrigerator cars, which were cooled with ice and refreshed at key points along the rail routes.

Under Harriman's leadership, the SP also won public acclaim and gratitude during two great natural disasters in the early 20th century. In 1905, after the Colorado River broke its banks during the construction of an irrigation works, SP began a successful two-year battle to return the river to its channel. Then in 1906, after the devastating April earthquake in San Francisco, SP evacuated 224,000 persons and rushed in huge quantities of relief supplies. Harriman even set up a public kitchen to help feed many of the hungry and homeless.

SP Fights for Survival

When Harriman died in 1909, he left the Southern Pacific an improved operating plant. However, he failed when it came to the system's balance sheet. Harriman had wheeled and dealt in a number of railroads, using the Union Pacific as a holding company, but the US Department of Justice did not look favorably upon his ambition to control the SP and the CP through the Union Pacific. Government lawyers filed suit to break up the two systems, and the case was settled five years later in the government's favor. On appeal, the Supreme Court upheld the government, forcing the UP to sell its interest in SP. The two railroads were again in competition, just as they had been in the early days.

The antitrust issue came to head again a few years later when the government ordered the SP to divest itself of its CP stock, and the Supreme Court upheld the order. The issue was sent to a district court for the cutting up of the Big Four's railroad empire.

By 1923, however, Congress had grown more sympathetic and came to the rescue of the system by revising the Interstate Commerce Commission (ICC) regulations to allow the ICC to approve the acquisition or control of one railroad by another—if it was in the public interest. Later, the ICC so ruled, allowing the SP to retain control of its CP stock.

The UP had complained for years that SP chose to send freight trains across the southwest on its own lines rather than share the business across the original transcontinental route. The ICC also ordered the SP and the UP to retain control of

financial success assured, UP directors authorized the issuance of $100 million in convertible bonds, and Harriman was told to use the funds raised from their sale as he saw fit. He used the $100 million to purchase a 46 percent share of the SP and took total control of the Central Pacific.

As soon as Harriman gained control of the railroad, he set to work updating and improving the SP system which had suffered a slight decline in the last years of Huntington's life. He saw to it that three big projects were completed. First, he ordered a 10-mile stretch of track between San Francisco and Los Angeles be straightened, thereby providing a water-level route in place of a steeply graded inland route. He then ordered construction of a 60-mile cutoff between Burbank and Montalvo in southern California. Both changes saved time and hence, money for the railroad.

The final project was the most difficult—the so-called Lucin Cutoff across the Great Salt Lake in Utah. At the time, it was considered an impossible engineering feat because of the length and unstable conditions under the lake, which required filling with thousands of tons of rock-fill before a wooden trestle could be erected across it. Yet completion of this project cut 44 miles off the old route north of Salt Lake, including that portion of the original transcontinental line at Promontory. Harriman spent more than $240 million improving the system between 1901 and 1909.

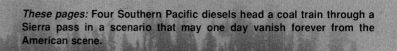

These pages: Four Southern Pacific diesels head a coal train through a Sierra pass in a scenario that may one day vanish forever from the American scene.

Southern Pacific 1904

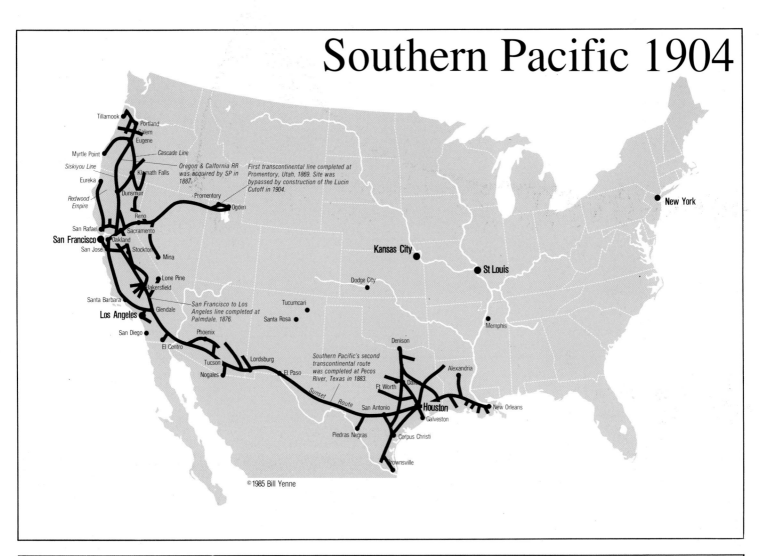

Tillamook
Portland
Salem
Eugene
Cascade Line
Myrtle Point
Siskiyou Line
Klamath Falls
Eureka
Dunsmuir
Redwood Empire
Reno
San Rafael
Sacramento
San Francisco
Oakland
San Jose
Stockton
Mina
Lone Pine
Bakersfield
Santa Barbara
Glendale
Los Angeles
San Diego
Phoenix
El Centro
Tucson
Nogales
Lordsburg
El Paso

Oregon & California RR was acquired by SP in 1887.

Promentory

First transcontinental line completed at Promentory, Utah, 1869. Site was bypassed by construction of the Lucin Cutoff in 1904.

Ogden

New York

Kansas City

St Louis

Dodge City

Tucumcari

Santa Rosa

Memphis

San Francisco to Los Angeles line completed at Palmdale, 1876.

Denison

Southern Pacific's second transcontinental route was completed at Pecos River, Texas in 1883.

Ft Worth
Dallas
Alexandria
Sunset Route
San Antonio
Houston
New Orleans
Galveston
Piedras Negras
Corpus Christi
Brownsville

© 1985 Bill Yenne

Southern Pacific 1984

Tillamook
Portland
Salem
Eugene
Cascade Line
Myrtle Point
Siskiyou Line
Klamath Falls
Eureka
Dunsmuir
Redwood Empire
Promentory
Reno
San Rafael
Sacramento
San Francisco
Oakland
San Jose
Stockton
Mina
Lone Pine
Bakersfield
Santa Barbara
Glendale
Los Angeles
San Diego
Phoenix
El Centro
Tucson
Nogales
Lordsburg
El Paso

Ogden

New York

Former Rock Island line between Tucumcari and St Louis acquired by Southern Pacific as a Cotton Belt operation in 1980.

Kansas City

St Louis

Dodge City

Tucumcari

Santa Rosa

El Paso & Southwestern RR was acquired by SP in 1924.

Memphis

St Louis Southwestern (Cotton Belt) acquired in 1932.

Denison

Alexandria

Ft Worth
Dallas
Sunset Route
San Antonio
Houston
New Orleans
Galveston
Piedras Negras
Corpus Christi
Brownsville

Southern Pacific of Mexico line was acquired in 1898, extended from Guaymas to Guadalajara in 1909, and sold to Mexican Government in 1951.

© 1985 Bill Yenne

Above: **Number 4449 in *Daylight* colors crosses the Mississippi River at New Orleans for the 1984 World Exposition.**

the Ogden Route as one line—neither railroad discriminating against the other—and SP was mandated to solicit as much business as it could generate from the region between Oregon and the Tehachapi Mountains.

The Southern Pacific survived World War II in a strong cash position and set about the task of carrying freight and passengers. The year 1945 saw SP officials embark on an ambitious plan to spend more than $2 billion to upgrade tracks and facilities. However, the post-war era turned out to be not profitable for America's railroads. SP fared better than most when Congress repealed low 'land-grant rates' for government traffic, enabling the SP to increase rates and improve revenues and earnings. But SP had a more difficult time competing against other forms of transportation that emerged in the 1960s and 1970s.

Deregulation

Famous passengers trains like *The Sunset Limited*—running between Los Angeles and New Orleans—and *The Coast Daylight* gave ground to automobiles and commercial jets. Later, with completion of the Interstate Highway System, SP also suffered a loss of business to the trucking industry.

SP was hard hit by the recession that struck the United States in 1982—the worst economic downturn since the Great Depression of the 1930s. Major industries, such as lumber in the Pacific northwest, minerals in the Pacific southwest and steel and heavy manufacturing, declined and did not regain economic health.

The End of the Line

The Staggers Act, signed into law by President Jimmy Carter, brought about the most sweeping reforms since the creation of the Interstate Commerce Commission in 1887. The reforms focused on ratemaking and allowed the marketplace rather than regulators to determine the cost of shipping goods by rail. The act permitted railroads to merge and consolidate, improving revenue by cutting duplicate services—a process that had been urged by outside experts for many years.

Taking advantage of the new business climate, Chicago-based Santa Fe Industries and Southern Pacific announced in 1983 that they were merging; the new system would be known as the Santa Fe Southern Pacific Railroad. The ICC, however, rejected the merger in an historic decision in the summer of 1986. Santa Fe Southern Pacific has appealed the ruling, and the two railroads are currently operating separately until the merger is approved.

Ironically, the ICC decision came as the parent company began painting both SP and Santa Fe locomotives with a new gold and red paint scheme. If the decision to keep the railroads separate is upheld, the photographs of the locomotives will become collector items.

If the appeal is granted, the name 'Southern Pacific' will disappear from the scene. No matter what happens, however, SP's legacy will continue for a long time. It is a name etched in the history of the Wild West.

UNION PACIFIC

Created by Presidential Signature

The Union Pacific (UP) Railroad traces its beginnings to the early days of the Civil War, when Congress passed the Pacific Railroad Act of 1862, establishing the UP as one of two companies to build the transcontinental railroad. Since that time, the UP has survived major wars, depressions and bankruptcies to become, in the 1980s, one of the largest and most successful railroads operating in the United States.

Today, the Union Pacific—a subsidiary of the Omaha-based Union Pacific Corporation—includes the Missouri Pacific, the Western Pacific and the Missouri-Kansas-Texas railroads, making it the third largest rail system in the nation. Every hour of the day the UP operates more than 200 trains over 21,500 miles of track. With one of the biggest equipment inventories in the nation, it has 2500 locomotives and 95,000 pieces of rolling stock.

The UP, the leading carrier of auto parts, coal, grain, forest products and trailer and container traffic, serves 10 of the nation's largest ports. In recent years, the railroad has been one of the leading innovators of 'double-stack' intermodal trains, capable of carrying twice as much cargo than ordinary flat cars by stacking containers two-high on flatcars. These special trains operate between major west coast ports such as Oakland and Long Beach and the midwestern markets.

Not to be outdone in the field of high technology, the UP was the first freight railroad to use fiber optic cables to provide communication services for its operations, allowing UP officials to transmit voice, video and computer messages between major cities served by UP trains.

Building Westward

The Pacific Railroad Act authorized the Central Pacific (later to be known as the Southern Pacific) and the Union Pacific railroads to build a link to California. The Central Pacific was designated to drive east from Sacramento, while the UP would drive west from the Missouri River.

The two railroads undertook construction at a time when pioneers walked or rode by horse or wagon train to get to California or Oregon. Under good conditions, the trek took up to six months, but conditions were rarely good. The journey

Opposite: This 1920 Union Pacific 0–6–0 is at the Railroad Museum in Sacramento. *Below:* US president Abraham Lincoln signed the UP into being.

had to be made in the harsh heat of summer to avoid getting trapped in deep winter snows in the Sierra Nevadas. Furthermore, hostile Indian attacks were always a threat.

Proposals to build a rail line to the Pacific came as soon as the earliest railroads began operating in the 1830s in the east. Recognizing the importance of trade between the United States and the Orient, Asa Whitney—involved in trading with China—went to Washington, DC in 1844 to try to convince Congress to sell him 78 million acres of government land at 16 cents per acre, to raise the capital necessary to build a Pacific railroad. He argued that such a transportation system would help open up the Pacific trade routes.

His proposal stirred great interest in the project, but little action, although Whitney traveled widely throughout the nation to promote his scheme, winning approval from 17 state legislatures. But he failed to gain support from US Senator Thomas Hart Benton of Missouri, who wanted to begin the Pacific railroad from St Louis in his home state. Congress disregarded Whitney's proposal in favor of Benton's, and after Whitney unsuccessfully tried to enlist British support, he gave up.

Whitney's extensive campaigning had one major effect. He got people thinking and talking about the project. Meanwhile, Benton arranged for a survey to be carried out by his son-in-law, John Fremont, the famous scout called 'The Pathfinder,' to determine the best route from St Louis.

Unfortunately, Fremont's survey of 1848 ended in disaster. Ten of his men were killed during the expedition, giving ammunition to those who opposed government support for the project. But Benton remained undeterred, convincing his fellow senators and representatives to set aside a 100-mile wide strip of government-owned land along the 38th parallel for a national railroad.

Above: This photo of Deep Cut Number One, west of Wilhelmina Pass, shows how the road was pickaxed and blasted down to grade. *Above right:* UP Loco Number 5 and the UP's photo car, complete with antlers. *Opposite:* Samuel B Reed, the UP's general superintendent of construction.

Debate continued with much talk and little action until in 1853 Congress instructed the War Department to determine the best and least costly route from the Mississippi River to the Pacific coast. Congress gave Secretary of War Jefferson Davis—later to serve as president of the Confederacy—$340,000 to conduct the survey. Five possible routes were eventually chosen and presented in a report to Congress. Later, portions of the routes were eventually followed by various railroads during the westward expansion.

The first, the so-called 'North Route,' ran between the 47th and 48th parallels, stretching a distance of 2025 miles from St Paul, Minnesota to Seattle, Washington. The cost was set at $141 million. Today it is one of the main lines of the Burlington Northern.

The second, known as the 'Central' or 'Overland Route,' extended for a distance of 2032 miles along the 41st and 42nd parallels from Council Bluffs to Benicia, California. The price was set at $131 million. The Central Pacific and the UP later followed sections of this route.

The third, called the 'Buffalo Trail,' followed the 38th and 39th parallels from what is now Kansas City to San Francisco for 2080 miles. The cost was never fixed because the survey party was massacred by Indians before they could complete the survey. Besides, the highest point along the way, reaching more than 10,000 feet in the Rocky Mountains, was deemed impossible for railroad construction. Yet today, sections of this survey are followed by the Denver & Rio Grande Western Railroad.

The fourth route, known as the 'Santa Fe Trail,' covered a distance of 2096 miles from Fort Smith, Arkansas through Santa Fe, New Mexico. It was estimated to cost more than $106 million, and sections of it were eventually followed by the Atchison, Topeka & Santa Fe Railway.

The fifth, known as the 'Southern Route,' ran for a distance of 2024 miles along the 32nd parallel from Fulton near Texarkana on the Arkansas-Texas border to San Francisco via El Paso, Fort Yuma and Los Angeles. At $90 million, it was the least expensive of the five, and would later become the main line of the Southern Pacific.

The Southern Route was favored by Davis and other southerners in government because they wanted southern states to benefit from the construction of a transcontinental railroad. Davis even excluded this route from the survey ordered by Congress in the hope that other routes would prove too costly or too difficult, leaving the Southern Route as the only alternative.

He eventually included the Southern Route in his report so that all routes could be evaluated equally. Later, the United States purchased land from Mexico (the Gadsen Purchase) along the US-Mexican border for the purpose of building a southern railroad. But the Civil War interrupted that effort, with Davis hastening south to serve as president of the secessionist states and Congress deciding to fix the route for a transcontinental railway north of the Mason-Dixon Line.

The route that was eventually chosen for the Pacific railroad was the one laid out by Theodore D Judah, a civil engineer who had even written and published a pamphlet on the subject, called 'A Practical Plan for Building the Pacific Railroad,' which he distributed in Washington. At the time the lawmakers were more concerned with the approaching clouds of civil war

than with a Pacific railroad, so Judah retreated back to California, where he found four Sacramento merchants—Collis Huntington, Leland Stanford, Mark Hopkins and Charles Crocker—who were prepared to help him build his dream: a Pacific railroad.

Construction Begins

Under the terms of the Pacific Railroad Act, the UP was to be awarded land grants and cash from the sale of 30-year US bonds to subsidize the cost of materials and construction. For each mile of track completed the railroads would be awarded one section of land 10 miles square in alternative sections on each side of the right-of-way. They also would receive a loan of $16,000 for each mile completed on the flat terrain, the $32,000 and $48,000 for each mile completed in more difficult terrain and mountains. Later, Congress was criticized for being too generous in handing out grants, but such aid was instrumental in helping to finance construction of the railroad and to settle the west.

Despite the promise of government land grants and cheap loans, the two railroads had to struggle to get the project underway. For one thing, because investors could make more money by investing in the war than in railroads, little capital was left. Also, materials became more expensive as the war raged because the Railroad Act stipulated that iron rails used in construction had to be American made, regardless of cost.

Disruptions surrounding the Civil War prevented the UP from breaking ground until December 1863, and actual work did not begin until December 1864 because UP could not raise sufficient capital. The UP's charter required raising $2 million in stock before beginning construction, but there were few

takers. By the end of 1864, the UP was still unable to lay tracks beyond Omaha City, Nebraska.

When groundbreaking was finally scheduled, officials held modest ceremonies at Omaha on the Missouri River. Yet within two years, it was clear that the concessions granted to the two railroads would not be sufficient. Thomas Durant, one of the principal organizers of the UP, and Collis Huntington, his counterpart from the Central Pacific, persuaded Congress to amend the Railroad Act of 1862. The original law had called for loans to be held up until track was completed, but Durant and Huntington were able to convince Congress to release two-thirds of the needed loans even before any track was laid. Congress also doubled the size of the land granted for each mile of track completed, from 10 square miles to 20.

Later, when even more financial aid was necessary, President Lincoln enlisted the help of Boston millionaire Oakes Ames, his brother Oliver and his well-heeled friends to invest in Durant's project. While the Central Pacific had its 'Big Four,' the Union Pacific had Thomas Durant, who got the project off the ground, took most of the original stock subscriptions in his new company, and then fought vigorously to retain control during construction. Durant made himself vice president, general manager and chairman of both the executive and finance committees of the UP and president of the Credit Mobilier of America, the financing arm of the railroad (while modestly declining, however, to take a salary).

A native of Massachusetts, Durant had attended medical school in New York, where he graduated with a degree in surgery. He soon abandoned medicine, however, in favor of working for an uncle who exported grain and flour in New York City, then began to speculate in railroad stocks. Discovering how profitable railroads could be, he moved from stock speculation to participation and became one of the builders of the Chicago & Rock Island Railroad. The Rock Island terminated at the Mississippi River, but Durant wanted to expand westward so he commissioned Major General Glenville Dodge, who would become chief engineer for the UP, to conduct initial surveys for his Mississippi & Missouri Rail Road—the first ever made across the state of Iowa. But the railroad, undercapitalized, went bankrupt and Durant returned east to push for passage of the Pacific Railroad Act.

While Durant was a shrewd promoter, he was also hard working and something of a perfectionist. He constantly prowled the tracks during construction to make sure the job

was completed the way he wanted. He could be dictatorial, but it was because he sought perfection. One newspaper reporter described him as a man whose 'mainspring seems to be not love of money for itself, or of notoriety in any sense, but a love for larger operations—a restless desire to be swinging great enterprises and doing everything on a magnificent scale.'

Durant was not the only man behind the success of the UP. There was also General Dodge who, when named chief engineer of the UP, was considered one of the most knowledgeable railroad engineers in the nation.

A native of Salem, Massachusetts, Glenville Dodge had studied civil engineering in Vermont with aspirations of one day building a railroad across the continent. After graduation,

Above left: Lover of large scale operations Thomas C Durant, the man who built the UP. *Below left:* A UP payday gathering at the paymaster's car at Promontory in 1869. The *General Sherman (above)* was the UP's first locomotive. *Below:* Grenville M Dodge, surveyor and chief engineer of the UP.

he took a job as a surveyor with the Illinois Central Railroad, where he met Durant.

Dodge was a colonel in the 4th Iowa Infantry when the war began in April 1861. He was promoted to major general on the strength of his skill in reconstructing and re-equipping railroads for the Union Army during the fighting. General Ulysses S Grant gave Dodge the task of repairing Southern railroads damaged in the fighting, and Dodge gained a reputation for engineering work on the Mobile and Ohio Railroad as well as lines around Nashville and Chattanooga in Tennessee and Decatur, Georgia.

In April 1863, Abraham Lincoln invited Dodge to the White House to ask advice on where to locate the eastern terminus of the Pacific railroad. Both agreed that Omaha was the proper place.

Dodge served out the war as commander of the Department of Missouri. Later, the Department of Kansas came under his control and, following the assassination of Lincoln in April 1865, Dodge was assigned command of the US military forces in Kansas, Nebraska, Colorado and Utah. A year later he had succeeded in putting down Indian uprisings under his command.Dodge was just 35 years old when he assumed his engineering duties in May 1866, but he had more than proven his skill in building railroads and bridges during the war, and his appointment came with the personal approval of President Lincoln. Those who knew Dodge said he acted quickly and decisively, reaching sound conclusions in the process.

He ran into problems with Durant as soon as he arrived in Omaha. Durant and his other investors wanted the UP to take the least direct course westward so that they could collect as much money as possible from land grants and bond sales. But Dodge won the argument for the most direct line possible after calling in Ulysses Grant to settle the dispute.

With the Civil War over and with capital and materials once again available, work began to pick up. By September 1866, more than 180 miles had been laid west of Omaha. After four years of struggle, the Pacific railroad was beginning to gather steam.

Although Dodge was chief engineer, the actual track work was carried out under the supervision of the Casement brothers, Daniel and 'General' Jack. Both were short, wiry, rugged men who were knowledgeable in railroad construction. Jack was only five-foot, four-inches tall and had served with General Sherman during the war, while younger brother Dan was just five foot high, but the two men between them had garnered 13 years of experience building railroads in the east before coming to the Union Pacific. Jack was the leader, carrying a pearl-handled Colt revolver on his hip to enforce the law. 'I depended on him for policing the line,' Dodge wrote of his charge. 'He was very prompt and active in such matters.' Dan meanwhile was the record-keeper and organizer.

Construction Gets Under Way

Before UP construction began in earnest in 1865, just 250 men worked on the project. Within a year of their arrival, Dodge and the Casement brothers had 10,000 men on the job, not to mention hundreds of horse and mule teams. The crews lived in boarding cars and tents kept at the back of track construction, moving everything forward every few days as construction on the track advanced.

These pages: **A UP woodburner pauses by the water tank at the Green River Bridge, near Citadel Rock (in the background) in the 1860s.**

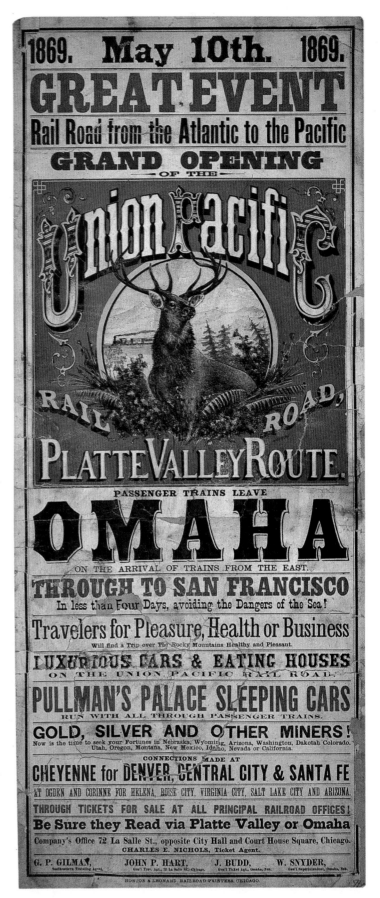

The track gangs, at first, could lay only three miles of rail each day. Later, when they had been on the job for a number of years, they could build as many as eight or nine miles of track in one day. The men were organized according to jobs performed. One gang first graded the track bed, while other gangs followed to put down ties, ballast and rail.

Bases for handling the materials were organized from 100 to 200 miles from the construction site. Many of those bases remain today—known today as the towns and cities of Fremont, Fort Kearny, North Platte, Julesberg, Sidney, Cheyenne, Laramie, Benton, Green River, Evanston & Ogden.

The Casement brothers worked from offices constructed on cars—simple 85-foot flat cars on which had been built an office, kitchen and mess hall. Other cars carried bunks three tiers deep with 1000 rifles stacked in the ceilings ready for hostile Indians. The rolling offices could hold up to 250 men. Another 750 men—graders, teamsters, herdsmen and cooks—camped in tents along the line.

The workmen included many Irish and Civil War veterans from both North and the South who labored for $3 a day, good money for those times. As they pushed across the Great Plains they picked up speed and ability in laying the tracks. But UP struggled to meet its payroll all during the years of construction.

The process of building a transcontinental railroad was deceptively simple. It appeared easy, but it was hard, heavy work requiring muscle and stamina. Crews rolled flat cars—each carrying a set number of rails along with the exact num-

ber of spikes to hold them down—up to the railhead. As soon as the ties were dropped into place, a dozen men hauled two rails from the car and dropped them onto the ties. Another crew then gauged and hammered down the rails while the rail gangs pulled the cars forward to begin the process again.

Work proceeded as fast as a man could walk, with 30 to 40 men hammering in spikes behind the rolling flatcar. It took 30 seconds to lay a rail. With two crews working side-by-side,

Facing page: These two handbills not only advertise the opening of UP rail routes, but tout the luxury and accomodations of the trains of the time, which included Pullman sleepers and Fred Harvey meals at stations.

Above: A movie set of an early UP station. Compare this rather cozy setup with the photo of the somewhat starker 'real thing' on pages 54–55. *Below:* An early 0–4–0 'pony' switcher locomotive.

The Golden Spike celebration: *Left:* Irish workers watch the approaching CP engine. *Above:* The UP (No 199, at right) and the CP (*Jupiter*, at left) meet.

four rails could be thrown down in a minute. Close behind came the gaugers, spikers and bolters, who finished up by hammering spikes—10 spikes to a rail, 400 rails to a mile—to hold the work in place. The iron rails used in construction of the transcontinental project were shipped in from Pittsburgh and other eastern steel mills and were half the weight and size of today's steel rails.

Working conditions were primitive. Small bands of Indians would attack the crews and burn the tracks to avenge the trespassing of their hunting territories. The workers gave them whiskey to keep them away, but sometimes had to fight them off with handguns and rifles.

Making the most trouble were the Sioux, Cheyenne and Arapahoe. The Sioux, who roamed north of the Platte and North Platte rivers, fought not only whites but other tribes as well. South and west of the Platte roamed the Cheyenne and Arapahoe. The Cheyenne could be peaceful, but Dodge believed that 'there were no friendly Indians.' He kept men on guard duty when the crews worked in hostile territory, and he was proven right.

The Sioux once captured a party of UP engineers in the Black Hills of Wyoming, then sent them to Dodge with an un-

friendly message: 'We do not want you here. You are scaring away our buffalo. Turn back or we will make war.' William F 'Buffalo Bill' Cody said the crews were not only frightening the buffalo, but were killing them off by the thousands. Indeed, within a few years the buffalo had all but disappeared from the Great Plains.

Men from the track gangs entertained themselves by wandering into makeshift towns for an evening of bad whiskey, dance-hall girls, crooked card games and hangovers. The girls, gamblers and bartenders followed the progress of the construction project as it advanced across the prairie and the Rockies.

Despite Indians, occasional cash shortages and hangovers, progress continued across the prairie, so that, by the end of 1868, UP crews had completed 450 miles of track westward from Omaha. By the next spring, construction crews were racing westward through Wyoming and Utah to earn UP its share of entitlements to the government land grants before meeting up with the competing Central Pacific crews.

In fact, the CP and UP became so intent on getting as much government land as possible that in the spring of 1869 they were even constructing parallel lines. Finally, Congress designated Promontory, Utah as the meeting point and the great project neared completion. On 10 May 1869, as UP's No 119 and CP's *Jupiter* locomotives came to a shuddering halt within

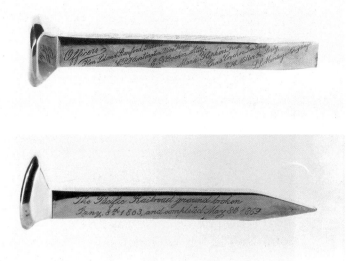

who assembled at Promontory spent more than a half-hour in front of the cameras for photographers to record the event.

Even before work was completed on the Pacific railroad, however, eastern newspapers began to question the expense and quality of Union Pacific's part of the project. Newspaper reporters visiting the construction site were especially critical of the quality of work performed and the materials used. One journalist inspecting construction first hand said it was 'third class' work. He said the public wanted the work completed rapidly and as economically as possible, yet done with quality.

The UP was criticized for using specially treated cottonwood for ties as well as for building inadequate culverts and weak bridges. Of the 2500 ties needed for each mile of track, only a third consisted of the harder woods, oak and walnut. Cottonwood was considered inferior because it quickly rotted and could not hold spikes.

Durant defended the use of the softer wood as a temporary expedient until the crews could replace them with oak and other hardwoods from the upper midwest. He insisted that proper construction techniques had been used when putting up the bridges and culverts. His explanations, however, did not settle the controversy, and the issue was debated long after completion of the railroad. But a greater scandal erupted in December 1867 when UP's financing company, Credit Mobilier, declared a more than 100 percent dividend to its investors. The outcry was shrill and immediate.

Durant and Ames believed that the money to be made in the project would not come from operation of the railroad but from its construction. They established Credit Mobilier to sell stock, then used the proceeds for construction. Critics claimed that the money was used to provide illegal kickbacks and under-the-counter payments to the promoters.

Congress set to work to find out how a company could make such high profits, especially when they came at the expense of the federal government. UP's books had already been inspected and deemed acceptable by the railroad commissioners. But Congress, unconvinced, was bent on uncovering wrongdoing.

A three-man commission appointed to investigate Credit Mobilier found that while the railroad was generally well constructed, a number of deficiencies did exist and would cost an estimated $6.5 million to correct. Meanwhile, the company's

a few feet of each other, the last rails were laid and the ceremonies began.

They were not without a few moments of comedy. Leland Stanford—then governor of California—attempted to drive in the golden spike prepared for the occasion with a sledge hammer. He was unsuccessful. When Durant tried to hit the spike, he too missed. Finally, diminutive Jack Casement stepped up, replaced the golden spike with an ordinary iron one, and hammered it into the Polish tie. The two locomotives then rolled slowly together to touch, signifying the end of the entire ambitious project.

The fabled golden spike had been donated by a San Francisco entrepreneur named David Hewes, who had made a fortune introducing steam shovels to San Francisco. He paid $25.25 to have $350 in gold hammered into the shape of a railroad spike, then placed it in a velvet box and presented it to Governor Stanford. Hewes did not want the event to occur without a special memento.

As soon as the ceremonies had ended, a telegram was sent to President Grant in Washington: 'The last rail is laid, the last spike is driven. The Pacific Railroad is completed. The junction point was 1086 miles west of the Missouri River and 690 miles east of Sacramento City.' The telegram was signed by Stanford and Durant and two other officers of the UP. Those

Above opposite: Two views of a replica of the Golden Spike, with pertinent data engraved thereon. *Above:* The illustrated interior of an 1880s-era Union Pacific dining car. *These pages, below:* This Union Pacific exhibition train is a reconstruction of the first UP passenger train west of the Missouri—locomotive, mail and baggage car, passenger coach, sleeper and business car.

These pages: In this photo from the 1870s, UP engine Number 23 sits on the main track in front of Wyoming Station. Number 23 was polished until every brass fitting gleamed in honor of this photo session 15 miles west of Laramie. A typical 4–4–0 'American' class locomotive, its looks were refined by the affixing of elk antlers to the engine's headlight. Note the old dog barking on the tender, and the lever action repeating rifle held by the man at front center.

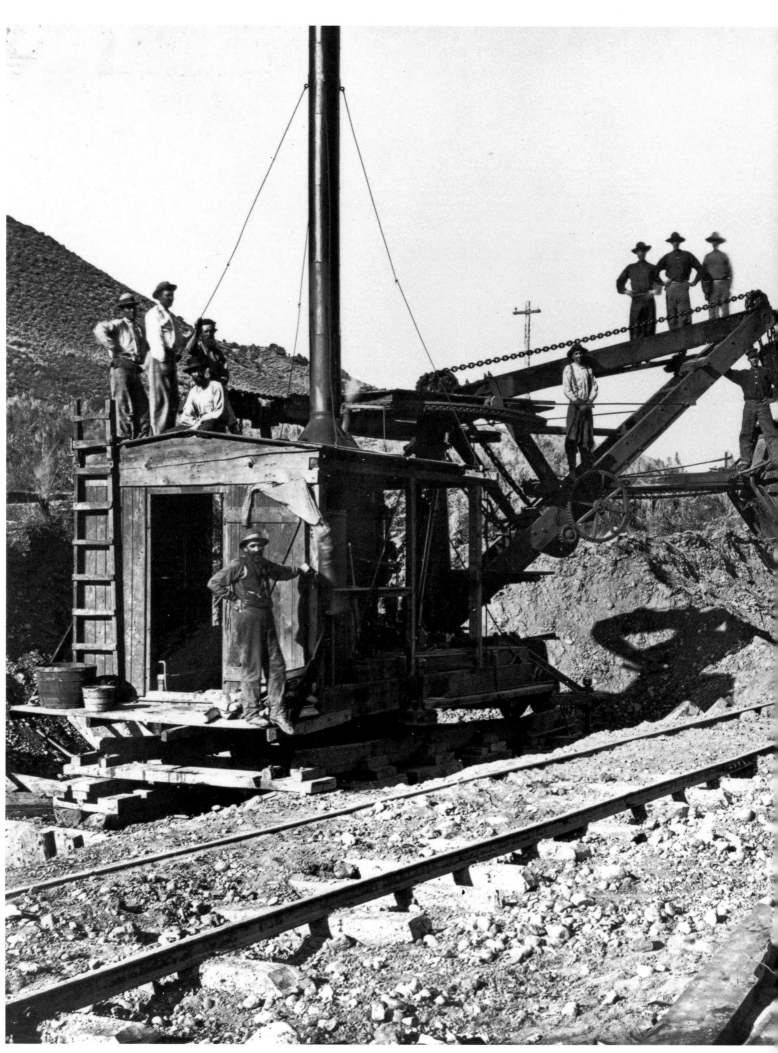

stockholders filed a lawsuit against Credit Mobilier, which led to the revelation that Oakes Ames had been distributing stock to influential congressmen where, it was said, 'it would do the most good.' However, Ames, who had made his money making shovels, was merely censured by Congress.

A number of years later, the author of a publication on the nation's railroads said, 'Americans do not build a railroad from Omaha to the Pacific in five years, making grade and laying track under almost impossible conditions while fighting savage tribes and prehensile politicians, without at least a trace of corruption.' Some observers said Ames had been made a scapegoat for his role in handing out stock in exchange for the votes necessary to get the railroad built. He was not any more corrupt, some critics noted, than the financial arm of the Central Pacific.

Others questioned the cost of the project, saying that the federal government had given away too much in land and cheap loans. Still others argued that with land costing the US government less than five cents per acre, it was well worth the price. Few in government mentioned the fact that the US retained the other half of the sections—land that would dramatically increase in value once the transcontinental railroad was completed. A report prepared in 1945 found that the government had received more than $900 million in payments for the federal lands that were granted under the Land Grant Acts.

While the scandal raged in Washington, the UP continued to expand its system. In September 1868 the railroad created a land department and undertook a campaign to encourage immigrants to relocate to areas served by the railroad. Soon, train loads of settlers began arriving, jumping off at stations so desolate they were little more than wood platforms in the middle of great plains and deserts.

However, successful completion of the transcontinental railroad did not prevent financial problems from pulling it into receivership, and the UP fell victim to the Panic of 1873 and was forced to declare bankruptcy. Like other railroads, the UP had been undercapitalized, leaving it in a weak financial condition. When business was good, the UP barely generated revenues sufficient to cover operating costs and return a profit to investors. When the economy dipped, as it did often in the turbulent second half of the 19th century, the UP generated losses and plenty of them.

At left: A steam shovel at Hanging Rock, Echo Canyon, in 1869. *Below:* Early UP locomotives used water-spouting guns to chase bison from the tracks.

After reorganization, however, the railroad expanded from its single line across the continent. In 1880, the Kansas Pacific and Denver Pacific railroads—and the cities of Kansas City and Denver—were added to the system. Then other branch lines were constructed. At the western end of the railroad, construction crews built lines into Idaho and Oregon and later to Seattle. The discovery of gold, silver and copper stimulated the construction of another line into western Montana.

The UP fell into bankruptcy again in the Panic of 1893 and was auctioned in Omaha on November 1897 to a group of investors headed by financier Edward H Harriman, who recognized the need to provide UP with the best he could afford. He set about inspecting almost every mile of track and, upon returning to New York, ordered a substantial rebuilding, including extensions of the Union Pacific into Utah. The cost was more than $25 million, and by the turn of the century Harriman announced that the rebuilding was complete. Within two years, despite the fact that loadings had declined 15 percent, he had doubled earnings.

When Harriman took over the Southern Pacific system in 1900, he merged the two giants; but the US Supreme Court ruled in 1913 that the Union Pacific had to divest itself of its SP stock, and the two railroads were separated.

When World War I broke out, the Union Pacific was ready to serve the nation. Unlike other railroads that struggled to meet the demands imposed by the war—antiquated locomotives and rolling stock and broken-down yards and trackage—Union Pacific trains and equipment, operating under the wartime command of the US Railroad Administration, performed without problems.

At top left: **UP Number 553, with engineer and oiler in 1882.** *Above left:* **The first UP railroad bridge at Omaha.** *Below:* **A UP Camel locomotive.**

The Depression era provided another test for Union Pacific, as the time came to make advances in motive power from steam to diesel. In 1934, UP introduced the nation's first streamlined diesel passenger train, *The City of Salina*, which toured the country on a grand publicity tour. It could speed along at 110 miles per hour on straight sections of track, and it hastened the arrival of diesel locomotives for passenger and freight service.

But the UP was not quite finished with steam. In 1941, Union Pacific received the first *Big Boy* locomotive, the world's most powerful steam locomotive at the time. It was one of the largest ever made, weighing more than 1.1 million pounds or 550 tons. Built to haul heavy loads up mountain grades, each locomotive could speed up to 80 miles per hour on level track. *The Big Boy* could consume 22 tons of coal and 22,000 gallons of water in an hour.

When World War II began, millions of tons of materials and hundreds of thousands of troops had to be moved in short order. Increases in freight loadings were staggering, but UP handled it without major problems and set records in the process.

On 20 October 1980, the Interstate Commerce Commission approved the application for merger of the Union Pacific, Missouri Pacific and Western Pacific railroads. Then in late 1986 the UP announced that it had filed an application with the ICC to merge with the Missouri-Kansas-Texas Railroad. The system now operated by Union Pacific spans the western two-thirds of the central United States, serving 22 states and with main lines extending from Chicago in the midwest to Los Angeles, Oakland and Seattle in the west and El Paso, Houston and New Orleans in the south.

Missouri Pacific

The Missouri Pacific played an important role in the development of western railroading. On 4 July 1851, ground was broken in St Louis for the construction of a Pacific railroad in early recognition of the need for a transcontinental line to the gold fields of California. A year later, the system's first locomotive, *The Pacific*, was off-loaded at the river wharf and pulled the first train ever operated west of the Mississippi.

As the Pacific railroad began operation, track was put down for another Missouri Pacific predecessor, the Iron Mountain Railroad, while other railroad projects in the region which eventually became part of the system were getting underway in Texas and Missouri. After the Civil War, the Pacific Railroad completed its line from St Louis to Kansas City, and daily service began between the two cities. Other railroad construction began, but despite ambitions of building to the

Above: The notorious, and unscrupulously successful, Jay Gould. Gould had a passion for making money, and had a gift—for gaining control of and exploiting railroads—with which to satisfy that desire. *At right:* The Los Angeles Union Pacific Terminal as it appeared in the late 1920s.

Pacific, Congress refused to grant aid as it had done for other railroads.

In 1879, New York financier and notorious 'robber baron' Jay Gould purchased controlling interest in the Missouri Pacific and took the title of president. Using the Missouri Pacific as a foundation, he forged a network of rail lines in the midwest, merging five smaller railroads into the Missouri Pacific.

Gould did not retain control of his new system for long. In 1885 he broke off the Texas & Pacific from the Missouri Pacific and, in 1888, allowed the Missouri-Kansas-Texas railroad properties to slip from his control. Of all the lines he added in that period, only the Iron Mountain remained. Between 1885 and 1892, however, officials constructed hundreds of miles of line into Colorado and Louisiana, and from 1909 to 1923 smaller subsidiaries were formally merged with the parent Missouri Pacific Railway.

Like most other lines, the Missouri Pacific experienced hard times during the Great Depression, even going into receivership in 1933 where it remained for 23 years. In the 1970s, the system took over the Chicago-based Chicago & Eastern Illinois Railroad and later the Texas & Pacific Railway. In 1980, stockholders approved a merger of the Union Pacific and Missouri Pacific, with the latter operating as the subsidiary.

62

Above: A load of ballast for the trestle pylons of the Lane Cutoff is discharged on target in 1908. *Below:* Union Passenger Station in El Paso in the 1950s. *Opposite:* The *City of San Francisco* operated over Chicago & Northwestern, Union Pacific and Southern Pacific tracks—hence it bore all three company logos.

The Manipulator

Before he became a railroad baron, Jay Gould had been a surveyor in Ohio, Michigan and New York and then worked in the tannery business—the nation's largest—in Pennsylvania. In the 1860s when he was in his late 20s, Gould left the leather business to speculate in stocks and bonds and small railroads, becoming a highly successful speculator. He even ran a railroad for a while—the Rensselaer & Saratoga Railroad in upstate New York. Gould was bound for bigger things, however.

In 1867, he and James Fisk took seats on the board of directors of the Erie Railroad. They, along with Daniel Drew, then proceeded to manipulate the company's stock, embezzle funds and use Erie resources for speculation in other ventures. When they had assumed control, the Erie boasted more than $16 million in cash reserves. Yet critics said they bled the Erie to the point where it was a decrepit old railroad. In 1868, competitor Cornelius Vanderbilt attempted to take control of the Erie, but was blocked when Gould, Fisk and Drew issued 50,000 shares of counterfeit stock to keep him at bay.

Vanderbilt called in the law, and the three were forced to flee to New Jersey to avoid arrest, carrying with them more than $6 million in cash. Later, they ventured to Albany, where they attempted to bribe members of the New York state legislature into legalizing the stock issue. They even had convinced one house to legalize the counterfeit stock, but reached a settlement with Vanderbilt before the legislation was completed.

Gould and Fisk, joined by Tammany Hall politicians Peter Sweeney and William 'Boss' Tweed, who were on the Erie

board, then forced Drew out of the Erie and began a spectacular series of frauds and complicated financial deals that made them millions of dollars while ruining many investors in the process.

They looted the Erie with huge stockwatering schemes, raided the credit, export and produce markets and, in 1869, attempted to corner the gold market. Gould's blatant attempt at profit-making resulted in the financial panic known as Black Friday, which forced President Grant to come to the rescue of the nation's economy by releasing $50 million in currency from the Treasury. Fisk was finally shot and killed by a disgruntled man in a love triangle, and Gould was ousted from the Erie Railroad board of directors in March 1872.

Gould soon turned to other railroads, though, leaving the Erie to go its own way and taking with him a personal fortune of more than $25 million. With this money, he began buying up large blocks of Union Pacific and became a director in 1874.

He maintained control of the UP for the next four years, buying control of the Kansas Pacific Railroad to expand his empire. As a director, he forced Union Pacific to merge with the Kansas Pacific at par value—much less than market value—by threatening to extend the Kansas line to Salt Lake City as a competitor. He was then able to sell his Kansas Pacific stock for more than $10 million. He also bought control of the Great Northern. His holdings were so vast that at one point he controlled more than one-half of all the railroad tracks in the southwestern US.

For a time he owned the *New York World* newspaper as well as the New York elevated railways and the Western Union Telegraph Company. When he died in 1892, he was one of the

At top: A Western Pacific Common Stock certificate. *Above:* Typical art deco station architecture of the 1930s. *Right:* An ad for GM diesel power.

richest men in the United States. Having started out as a blacksmith and clerk in a country store, Jay Gould let little interfere with his passion for making money, most of it through the ownership of railroads.

Western Pacific

The Western Pacific Railroad was organized in 1903 to run from San Francisco through California's Feather River Canyon and Beckworth Pass to Salt Lake City, where it was to connect with Jay Gould's Rio Grande-Missouri Pacific System. Work did not get underway until January 1903 when the first spike was driven at Oakland, California. Three years later, the final spike was driven on a steel bridge across Spanish Creek near Keddie, California. Service began two months later. This was

A NEW DAY DAWNS IN RAILROADING

War traffic has more than doubled the volume of freight hauled by the Western Pacific Railroad from Salt Lake City to San Francisco. Wherever the going is toughest on this rugged route, General Motors Diesel freight locomotives have kept this vast stream of vital munitions moving steadily.

AMERICAN EXPRESS TRAIN.

A crack "Express Train" of 1865 as pictured by Currier & Ives. Four years later an important new era began when the first railroad linked the Atlantic and Pacific.

Throughout history, wars have set up new milestones of transportation progress. And with this war, it is the General Motors Diesel Locomotive that is ushering in the new era. What advances the future will bring are already apparent in the present performance of these locomotives and the way they are helping to meet the abnormal demands upon the railroads today.

KEEP AMERICA STRONG · BUY MORE BONDS

War building is being rushed ahead with reliable General Motors Diesel power. In the days to come this dependable, economical power will be ready to do the hard jobs of peace.

GM GENERAL MOTORS **DIESEL POWER**

LOCOMOTIVES.....................ELECTRO-MOTIVE DIVISION, La Grange, Ill.

ENGINES..150 to 2000 H.P...CLEVELAND DIESEL ENGINE DIVISION, Cleveland, Ohio

ENGINES.....15 to 250 H.P......DETROIT DIESEL ENGINE DIVISION, Detroit, Mich.

the same year that the line was sold in foreclosure and re-emerged as the Western Pacific Railroad Company.

The Feather River is a spectacular route, providing passengers with sweeping vistas of the Sierra Nevadas. The line consists of 41 steel bridges and 44 tunnels as it crosses from Sacramento on the way to Salt Lake City. It was chosen originally because it is 2000 feet lower than the Donner Pass used by Southern Pacific.

In 1915, the Rio Grande defaulted on its obligations and the Western Pacific went into receivership. A year later the line reorganized, and Gould lost control. In 1928 the Western Pacific acquired the lines of the Sacramento Northern Railway, but again fell into receivership in 1935. It emerged from bankruptcy in 1945 and operated independently until 1980 when Union Pacific acquired the line.

Missouri-Kansas-Texas Railroad

In late 1986, the Union Pacific Corporation filed application with the ICC to acquire the 3100-mile Missouri-Kansas-Texas Railroad from Katy Industries for approximately $110 million. The UP also assumed more than $256 million in debts. UP executives said they decided to seek a merger because of their concern over the future of KMT's tracks.

The KMT, or 'the Katy,' will be merged into the 21,500-mile Union Pacific Railroad when approved by federal regulatory agencies. The Katy operates in some of the same geographical areas as the UP, Burlington Northern, Southern Pacific, Santa Fe and Kansas City Southern railroads. The merger includes part of the Rock Island line from Salina south to Dallas.

UP executives have long considered the Katy a vital part of Union Pacific's main route between Kansas and Texas because of trackage rights agreements. UP has trackage rights on 380 miles of the Katy's lines, while Katy has rights on some of UP's lines. Executives said the merger will guarantee them key routes between the midwest and the Gulf of Mexico.

The Katy operates primarily between the Gulf Coast at Galveston and Omaha/Council Bluffs; it carries mostly grain and coal, along with automobiles, steel products and chemicals.

The KMT began as the Union Pacific Southern Branch, with no connection to the UP. Organizers wanted to build a line from the Port of New Orleans to the northern Kansas border. Supported with government land grants, construction got

Below: A Union Pacific coal train loads up at the Prospect Point Mine. *At right:* Union Pacific yards and shops; Omaha is in the background.

Above: A Union Pacific *California Zephyr* passenger service ad of 7 April 1951. *At right:* A triple header Union Pacific freight train featuring UP diesels 6036, 6000 and 6056 bears its load under sunny western skies. The Union Pacific continues to ride the rails of our nation's west.

Above: Yesterday's dispatchers worked with levers and wires: contemporary dispatchers such as this man at North Platte, NE work with computers.

underway in 1869 and reached the southern Kansas border, then was allowed to extend into the territory known today as Oklahoma.

The company acquired a smaller railroad running through Sedalia, Missouri and changed its name to the Missouri-Kansas-Texas Railroad at the time. After reaching Denton, Texas, it battled for the rights to a crossing at Vinita, Oklahoma against the Atlantic & Pacific Railroad. Then in 1873, Jay Gould acquired control, pushing the line through to Dallas in 1881, the first railroad to enter Texas from the north. In ensuing years, the KMT bought two other lines—the Galveston, Houston & Henderson and the International & Great Northern.

It was during this era that Gould's midwestern railroads—including the St Louis & Iron Mountain, the Missouri Pacific and the Texas & Pacific—all went bankrupt. As a result, Gould was ousted as a controlling director of the KMT.

A Texas holding company was created to comply with a law which said that railroads operating within the state had to maintain offices there. But the KMT remained in control of creditors until 1910. Then the Texas Central was acquired along with two other lines operating in Kansas.

The owners changed the name to the Missouri-Kansas-Texas in 1823 after reorganization. Like many other railroads

in the period after World War II, the Katy, unable to compete successfully against long-haul trucks and other railroad competitors, declared bankruptcy in the 1950s. The road was reorganized and restored to profitability in the 1970s, but it has struggled in recent years in the wake of deregulation.

The UP had reached an agreement in 1985 with Katy Industries to acquire the KMT, but Katy was unable to obtain the specific number of registered certificates that had been issued when the road was in reorganization in 1958.

The name of the Missouri-Kansas-Texas Railroad was associated with some of the most famous outlaws in the days of the Old West. For hundreds of miles, the Katy followed the course of the old cattle trails that had been made famous in frontier lore. More than once, Katy trains were the victims of such men as Jesse James and the Younger brothers, not to mention Sam Bass and the Dalton Gang. The last robbery took place in 1923 when the Spencer Gang stopped a train near Okesa, Oklahoma and took more than $21,000 from a mail car. It was not a successful gambit, however, for every one of the gang members was killed or captured.

The Classic Union Pacific and Western Pacific Routes

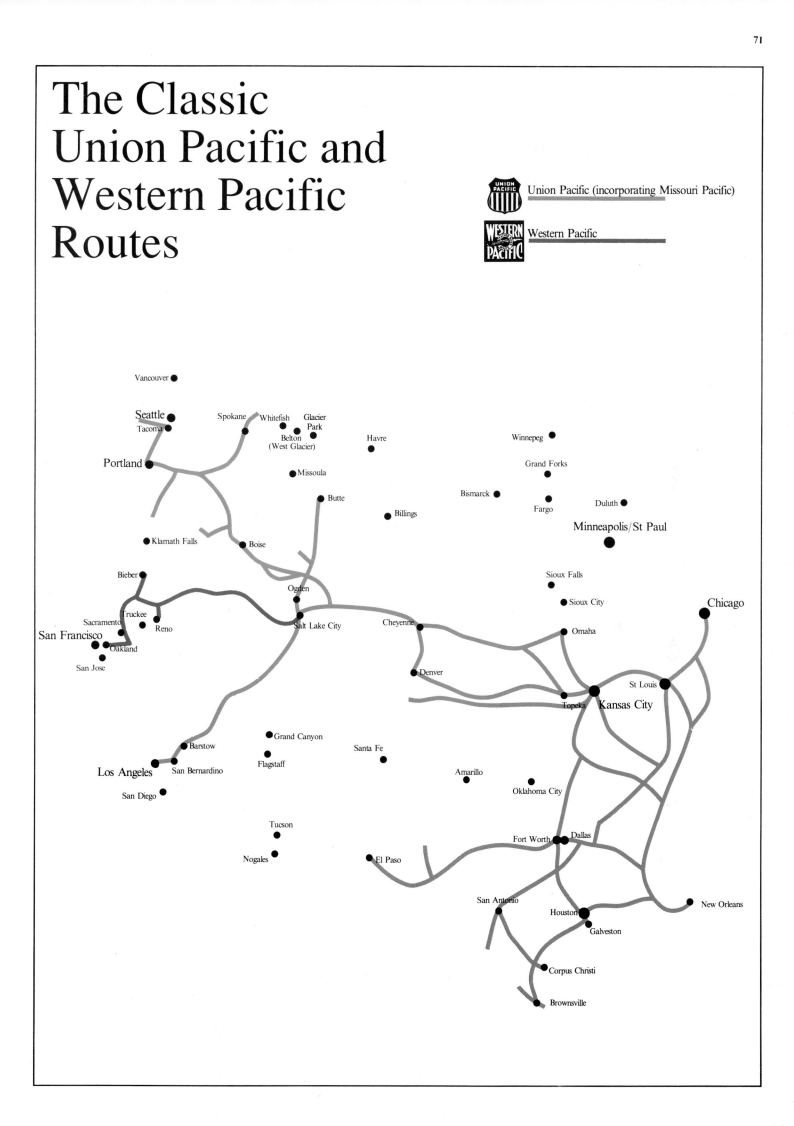

Union Pacific (incorporating Missouri Pacific)

Western Pacific

SANTA FE

Organized in the Wild West

The Santa Fe Southern Pacific Corporation represents the combination of two great railroads of the Old West—the San Francisco-based Southern Pacific Railroad and the Chicago-based Atchison, Topeka & Santa Fe Railway. While the Interstate Commerce Commission rejected a proposed merger of the two lines in the spring of 1986, the rejection has since been appealed.

The Santa Fe currently operates more than 12,000 miles of track over 13 states in the west and midwest. It deploys a fleet of more than 1800 locomotives and more than 52,000 freight cars. The Atchison, Topeka & Santa Fe Railway Company, best known as the Santa Fe, was organized in Topeka, Kansas in 1872 as the Atchison & Topeka Railroad. The Santa Fe has long been known for excellent freight and passenger service, a reputation that continues to this day.

Within a few years, tracks were extended to the Colorado border, then onward to Santa Fe, New Mexico. In the 1880s, the Santa Fe's tracks reached Los Angeles. Along with the Southern Pacific, the Santa Fe was instrumental in opening and settling vast tracts of land around Los Angeles in southern California.

By the turn of the century, the Santa Fe had stretched its reach northward to include Richmond, California on the San Francisco Bay where a yard and terminal are currently maintained. The Santa Fe also branched northeastward to Chicago, where company headquarters are now located. For a short time in the early part of the century, the Santa Fe merged with the St Louis Railway & San Francisco (the 'Frisco' Lines).

For nearly 100 years, the Santa Fe set the national standard for comfort, luxury and speed in passenger service. It also established records for rapid freight deliveries for commercial and industrial customers.

The Santa Fe has long been famous among rail fans and locomotive buffs as a railroad willing to experiment with new locomotives and rolling stock. It has never been satisfied with its current level of service to passengers and has always been willing to consider new equipment and advanced technologies. As a consequence, the traveling public has benefited.

In the days of steam, it was one of the first railroads west of the Mississippi to put articulated locomotives onto its main lines. This locomotive was a giant 2–10–10–2 with a hinged boiler that could pull heavy loads, as well as move quickly along the tracks. The Santa Fe was also one of the first railroads to operate steam trains over long distances. Its 4–8–4 locomotives used for passenger service could operate between Los Angeles and Kansas City without being changed.

Opposite: **A Santa Fe triple header freight rounds a curve into a straight stretch.** *Below:* **Southern Pacific (left) and Santa Fe engineers shake hands, symbolizing the 1983 merger of their parent companies.**

Above: The birthplace of the Santa Fe Railway at Atchison, Kansas; the humble little structure where Cyrus Holliday *(right)* organized the AT&SF.

With the introduction of diesel locomotives in the 1930s, the Santa Fe pioneered the changeover for passenger and freight operations. In 1935 it was the first railroad to use diesels, they pulled its famed *Super Chief* streamlined passenger trains from Chicago to Los Angeles and continued to set the pace for passenger service over the next three decades.

The Super Chief, one of the best-known passenger trains in the world, was used extensively by Hollywood motion picture stars and other celebrities. It succeeded *The Chief,* an all-steam train that ran between the Windy City and Los Angeles beginning in 1923. The all-Pullman *Super Chief* was followed by *El Capitan,* an all-coach streamlined diesel train inaugurated between LA and Chicago in 1938.

Even though Santa Fe offered the best passenger service in the world, however, it too eventually succumbed to the popularity of the personal automobile and the passenger plane. Santa Fe surrendered its passenger service to Amtrak in 1973.

Holliday Has a Dream

The early Santa Fe was the vision of Cyrus Kurtz Holliday, a Pennsylvanian who traveled to what is now Kansas in 1854 and laid the foundations of the Santa Fe before the Civil War. Holliday wanted to build a railroad from Topeka to Santa Fe, New Mexico to serve the entire region between those communities. He secured a charter in 1859 for his railroad— which he and his fellow investors modestly called the Atchison & Topeka Railroad—and gave himself the title of president.

Holliday believed Kansas would soon be settled and developed into a great region of agriculture and commerce. His dream did not appear realistic at the time, however, because Kansas was then so wild and unsettled—the same territory featured in the Wild West dime novels of the 1880s. But he knew that when settlers came to farm the fertile, cheap lands, the territory would grow rapidly.

Beyond Kansas lay the fabled city of Santa Fe, once part of the Spanish empire, but seized in 1846 for the United States during its war with Mexico. In Holliday's time it was already a bustling center of trade and farming, and Holliday wanted to replace the wagons that lumbered along the old pack-and-cattle Santa Fe trail with locomotives and freight cars.

Holliday was as much a part of the history of Kansas as the railroad he established. He joined the Free State Party, and when the settlers decided that the territory needed a state capital, Holliday helped to stake out what is now the city of Topeka. Later, after Kansas was admitted to the Union in January 1861, he attended the state constitutional convention.

Holliday set about to build his railroad, but was unable to attract investors until 1863 when Congress came to his rescue. In an effort to keep Kansas in the Union during the Civil War, Congress granted the Santa Fe three million acres of land, in alternate sections, to help finance and spur construction, just as it had helped the Union Pacific and Central Pacific lines build the transcontinental railroad. Congress put one major stipulation on

CYRUS K. HOLLIDAY
1826 — 1900
PIONEER AND BUILDER

FOUNDER AND MAYOR OF TOPEKA.
INFLUENCED THE SELECTION OF THIS CITY
AS THE CAPITAL OF KANSAS.
ORGANIZED THE ATCHISON, TOPEKA AND
SANTA FE RAILROAD COMPANY. OBTAINED
THE ORIGINAL CHARTER IN THE YEAR 1859.
PROMOTED THE EARLY DEVELOPMENT OF
KANSAS AND THE ENTIRE SOUTHWEST.

the land grants, however: that the Santa Fe would have to reach the Colorado border within 10 years to take title to the lands which they had been granted.

Like other western railroads, the Santa Fe found it difficult to raise adequate financing during the Civil War years. Yet Holliday remained optimistic and eventually, bolstered by support from the federal government, the Santa Fe's stockholders met and changed the name of the line to the Atchison, Topeka & Santa Fe Railway (ATSF).

Construction got under way in the fall of 1868, after local newspapers advertised for 500 men to work on the fledgling rail lines at the rate of $1.75 a day. During groundbreaking ceremonies, Holliday predicted that the Santa Fe would one day reach the Pacific and the Gulf of Mexico. His prediction came true within the next quarter century.

By 1869 the Santa Fe was operating 28 miles of track, and by 1871 track gangs had reached the notorious Dodge City, where arguments were often settled with guns. Dodge City and other cattle towns along the Kansas frontier were important to the Santa Fe, as they served as railheads for the large herds of Longhorn cattle driven up from Texas via the 'Old Chisolm Trail.' Until then the Kansas Pacific Railroad had enjoyed a monopoly on the cattle trade to Chicago. Now the Santa Fe wanted to cross Kansas south of Abilene to take some of Kansas Pacific's business.

In the early 1870s, these towns also served as major shipping points for buffalo hides. The enormous buffalo herds of the great plains were especially bountiful in Kansas, but with the coming of the railroads they were doomed. Buffalo robes and coats were highly fashionable in the eastern US and

Europe, and so much money could be made in hides that professional hunters undertook a wholesale slaughter of the buffalo.

Even the Santa Fe train crews and passengers took part, shooting buffaloes from passenger cars and locomotives simply for sport, while hundreds of tourists paid to take these excursion tips and killed thousands of buffaloes themselves. Yet it was the professional hunters who were mainly responsible for destroying the great herds. They killed the beasts by the millions, stripping off their hides, leaving the carcasses to rot, and shipping the hides and bones east to make coats and fertilizer. With the near-extinction of the buffalo, the range cattle industry began to prosper, bringing the ATSF a large share of the cattle business.

The Santa Fe track gangs continued working westward until they reached the Colorado border in late 1872, well ahead of the deadline set by Congress (and three years after completion of the transcontinental railroad). Like other western railroad employees, ATSF track gangs consisted of Civil War veterans—mostly Irish—and local farm boys, who drove teams of horses and mules.

The men did not have the best of working conditions. In fact, the weather could be miserable. In summer, the gangs labored under a hot, pounding sun, and in winter they faced freezing rain and snow. They lived in construction camps, slept in sheds built of scrap lumber, and existed on harsh food such as beans, salt pork, bread and sorghum. For meat they ate buffalo slaughtered by the professional hunters hired by the railroad. Construction camps followed the railhead as it moved westward. With the camps came professional gamblers and prostitutes who set up shop in makeshift tents.

It was cattle drivers, the cowboys of the frontier—not Indians—who were the worst threat to the workmen. These drivers and the railroad workers did not mix easily in the dance-halls and saloons. They often argued and fought, which sometimes led to injury and death.

As track construction progressed westward, the Santa Fe discovered that Kansas did not have enough people to serve the farmers, there could be no freight and no passenger business. Without people to farm the land, and without towns to generate business. So the Santa Fe Railroad set about to bring settlers to the region, opening a land department to publish

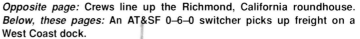

Opposite page: Crews line up the Richmond, California roundhouse. *Below, these pages:* An AT&SF 0–6–0 switcher picks up freight on a West Coast dock.

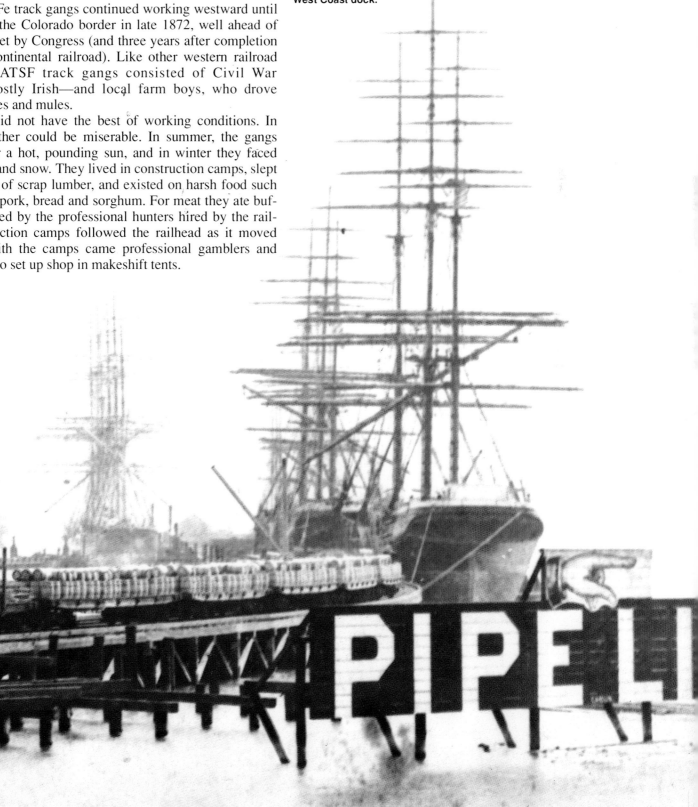

booklets and pamphlets to lure new settlers. In Europe, meanwhile, agents were hired to find people willing to emigrate to the US at special fares.

Santa Fe's immigration program got off to a shaky beginning. Kansas suffered through several grasshopper plagues in the late 1870s and through two serious droughts in 1879 and 1880. The crops withered, and thousands of farm animals died. The grasshoppers finally became so dense on the prairie that farmers could find no footing with which to work their horse teams. The Santa Fe trains were slowed, then brought to shuddering stops, when the pulp of smashed grasshoppers grew too slippery to allow traction. As thousands of people abandoned Kansas for other sections of the country with less grasshoppers and plenty of water, such natural disasters plunged the ATSF into the red.

Eventually, though, the grasshoppers disappeared and the rains returned, enabling the Santa Fe to recover financially and to continue its westward expansion. During this period of tribulation, the Santa Fe established a reputation as a well-managed company. A railroad magazine of the period even said it was 'one of the best roads west of the Mississippi.'

Wars in the Canyons of Colorado

The ATSF reached the Kansas-Colorado border in 1872, one year ahead of the 10-year deadline set by Congress to claim title to the land grants. Continued progress also set the stage for a showdown with another competitor, the Denver & Rio Grande (D&RG) Railroad, which had grand expansion plans of its own in Colorado.

William Jackson Palmer, who had been a Union cavalry general in the Civil War, organized the Denver & Rio Grande in 1870 to build southward from Denver to El Paso and then on to Mexico City. Palmer wanted to push his railroad into New Mexico as much as the ATSF wanted to reach Pueblo and Canyon City, already served by the D&RG.

By this time, Boston financiers Thomas and Joseph Nickerson had wrested control of the ATSF from Holliday (although he continued as secretary of the board of directors). These two brothers recognized the need to expand the business of the rail-

Below: A Santa Fe 0–4–0 switch engine on the waterfront in the San Diego of the 1880s. *At right:* An AT&SF passenger train at rest atop the Canyon Diablo Bridge in Arizona. The 2–4–0 American engine, by its slim smokestack, is a coal burner.

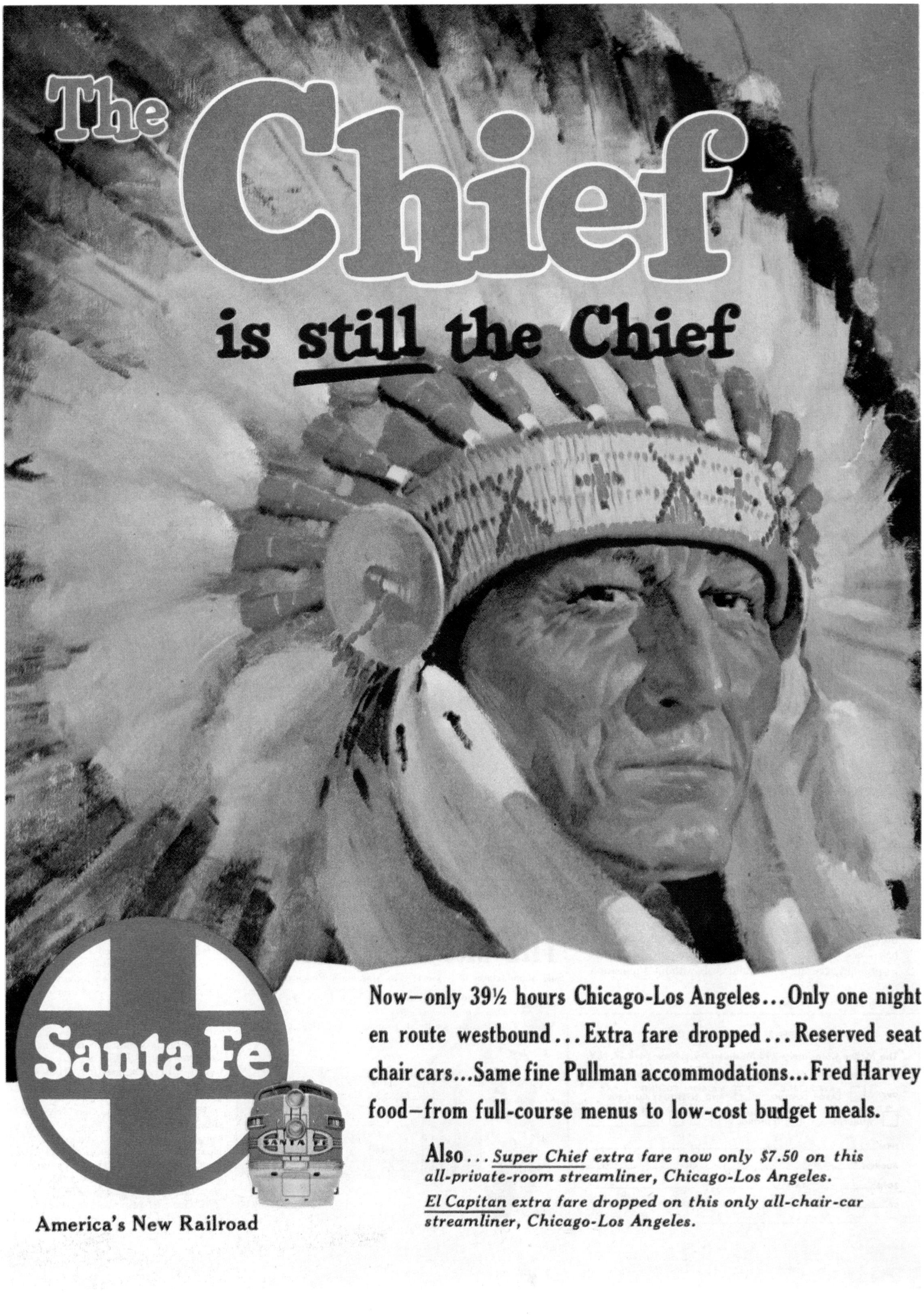

The Chief
is still the Chief

Santa Fe

America's New Railroad

Now—only 39½ hours Chicago-Los Angeles...Only one night en route westbound...Extra fare dropped...Reserved seat chair cars...Same fine Pullman accommodations...Fred Harvey food—from full-course menus to low-cost budget meals.

Also... *Super Chief extra fare now only $7.50 on this all-private-room streamliner, Chicago-Los Angeles.*

El Capitan extra fare dropped on this only all-chair-car streamliner, Chicago-Los Angeles.

road beyond carrying cattle and buffalo hides. They wanted to generate revenue from the various types of mining opportunities available in the Rocky Mountains of Colorado.

Palmer did not want to build a railroad competing against the Santa Fe, so he traveled east to persuade the new owners of the ATSF to cooperate in building one line. But his mission failed, setting up a confrontation for control of two important mountain passes—the Raton Pass from Colorado into New Mexico and the Royal Gorge in southern Colorado.

The first clash came in early 1873. Legal rights to the 8000-foot Raton Pass, located 15 miles south of Trinidad, Colorado, were ambiguous. Both railroads claimed title, although Thomas Nickerson did not see the urgency of crossing the pass to get to Santa Fe.

Wagon traffic between Santa Fe and Colorado was not that heavy, and Nickerson did not believe that the line would support a rail service. But Holliday convinced Nickerson and others on the ATSF board of directors of the need to expand into New Mexico.

Nickerson sent survey crews south to where Palmer had already ordered surveys. Nickerson leased the rights to construct the new line over the pass to a new railroad, the Canyon City and San Juan. Yet the D&RG and the Santa Fe were not the only railroads battling for rights to New Mexico.

The Southern Pacific, under CP Huntington's shrewd leadership, was trying to stop the ATSF and the D&RG. Thomas Nickerson had ordered General Manager William Barstow Strong to approach the New Mexico state legislature to negotiate the required rights to build rail lines in the state. When Strong reached Santa Fe, however, he discovered that Southern Pacific representatives had beat him there.

The SP men had persuaded the lawmakers to require that the boards of the railroad operating in New Mexico be dominated by state residents. In addition, the law required the railroads to

At left: This 20 March 1954 advertisement for Santa Fe's *Chief* and *Super Chief* passenger trains touted Pullman cars and Fred Harvey meals, and evidenced the Santa Fe's institutionalized 'Old West' motifs. *Below:* Work begins on 1 January 1887 for the Chicago, Santa Fe & California's Iowa leg.

demonstrate that they possessed 10 percent of the building costs before starting work, which would make construction impossible for the Santa Fe.

Strong was not to be deterred, however. He stalked the halls of the state legislature, seeking a way to get around the law, and he found that the SP agents had left one loophole. They had neglected to get the New Mexico lawmakers to repeal the old law. Still in force therefore and superceding the new law, the old legislation allowed the Santa Fe to proceed without meeting the new requirements! Strong immediately created a new corporation—the New Mexico & Southern Pacific Railroad Company—to build from the Raton Pass to the Arizona border. He even convinced the lawmakers to exempt the new line from taxes for six years.

With business in Santa Fe completed, the stage was set for a construction battle with the D&RG for the Raton Pass. Strong returned to Kansas and instructed his crews to prepare to build a line across the Raton Pass—using force if necessary. He took a train to Trinidad where he recruited a small army of men and armed them with rifles and shovels. Palmer, on his side, had already recruited armed men to fight for control of the pass.

The opposing forces arrived at the mouth of the Raton Pass on the same day in 1873. Men from the two railroads growled at each other, but the expected fight did not erupt. The Santa Fe, having arrived just minutes ahead of the D&RG, took control of the Raton Pass, and its track crews went to work the next day.

On 7 December 1878, the first train traveled over Raton Pass by means of a switchback. The next year, crews bored a 2000-foot tunnel through the summit, reducing the maximum grade from 316 feet per mile to 185. The Santa Fe finally had reached New Mexico—after more than a decade.

The contest for Raton Pass was not the last time the two railroads would battle over Colorado real estate. Later, ATSF and the Rio Grande fought for control of the Grand Canyon of the Arkansas (called the Royal Gorge), a narrow rift 3000 feet deep through granite Rockies west of Pueblo, leading to lucrative coal fields.

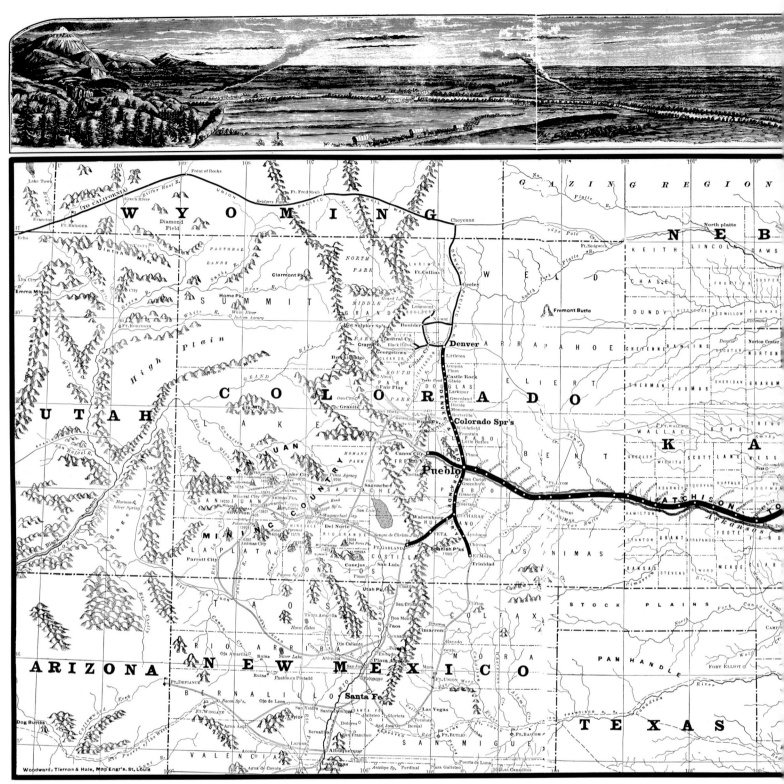

Once again, Strong ordered armed men into action and sent them to the Royal Gorge to prevent D&RG crews from advancing. He also ordered one of his engineers, William R Morley, to round up reinforcements from Canyon City. Morley, however, could not travel on D&RG trains, so he had to ride 63 miles on horseback to get help. Morley's horse died from exhaustion but he saved the day for Santa Fe.

Meanwhile, Palmer and 200 armed men boarded a train and traveled to the mouth of the gorge, prepared to do battle. Morley led his own armed group back to the mouth of the canyon to confront Palmer and told the band of men recruited by the Denver & Rio Grande that he would use all necessary force to stop them.

'We got here first, and we're building the Canyon City & San Juan Railroad through the Arkansas,' he shouted. 'Anyone interfering with this work is liable to stop a bullet between the eyes.' They decided not to fight, allowing the Santa Fe to take control of the pass.

Thwarted, Palmer went to court to stop the Santa Fe from encroaching further into his domain, but his legal fight was unsuccessful. The court gave the Santa Fe a lockhold lease on the D&RG, and the ATSF assumed operational control of the competing line.

Palmer returned to the courts, claiming that the Santa Fe was violating its lease agreement by raising the rates on the Rio Grande line prohibitively high, thus diverting traffic to the Santa Fe and attempting to bankrupt the D&RG. When the Colorado Supreme Court returned control of the embattled line to Palmer in June 1879, he sent armed detachments to the Royal Gorge Canyon to block Santa Fe from operating there.

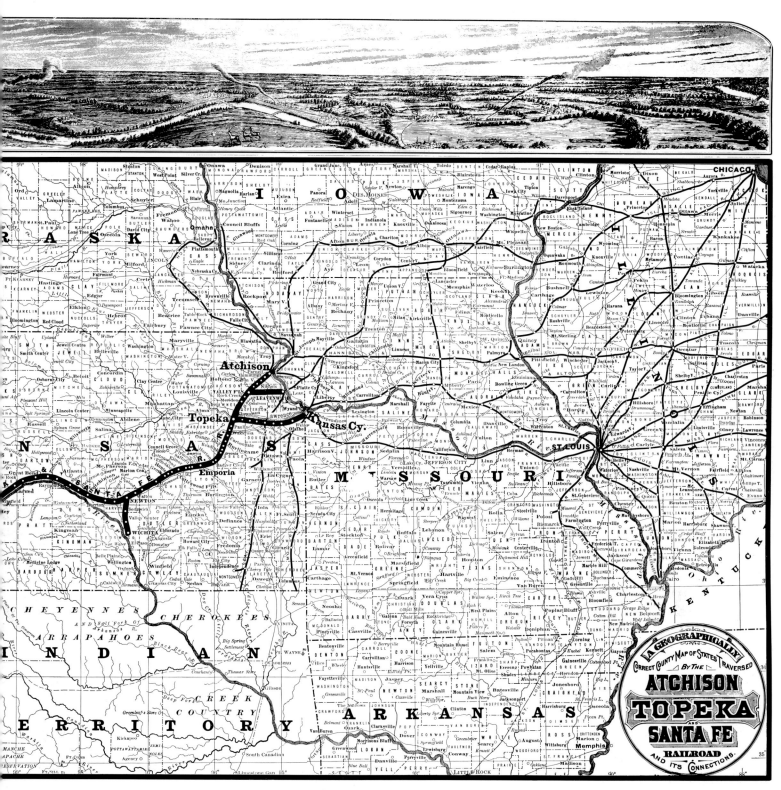

The men arrived and ordered Santa Fe to stop work 'by authority of the Supreme Court and the 50 rifles you see here.'

While heavily armed sheriff's deputies distributed the court order to Santa Fe employees operating the D&RG trains and depots, Rio Grande employees commandeered a Santa Fe train, retaking stations from El Moro to Pueblo, and open warfare soon erupted between employees from the two lines. Santa Fe crews operating trains on the Rio Grande tracks were attacked and beaten and their families were threatened.

The showdown came at Pueblo, where Rio Grande crews were met by Bat Masterson, the famous Dodge City marshal. Masterson, who boasted a long list of legally justified killings, had been imported to protect Santa Fe property. He had with him a gang of armed men to keep Santa Fe property safe from the Rio Grande employees.

As the Rio Grande train approached, loaded with armed men, Masterson ordered his gang to surround the roundhouse where the train would stop at Pueblo, and told them to prepare to shoot. But no shots were fired. When the Rio Grande boys saw Masterson and his men with their revolvers, carbines and shotguns drawn, the threat was more than enough to stop a fight.

Under a white flag of truce, leaders from the two armed camps discussed the issue. The Rio Grande forces decided to buy off Masterson, thus retaking the Pueblo roundhouse without violence. Masterson and his men were allowed to lay down their arms and leave peaceably under the protection of law officers.

The war was not yet over. The dispatcher's office remained in the hands of Santa Fe men, who were not about to give ground. When Rio Grande men assaulted the office with a barrage of bullets, two men were killed and two were injured.

Finally the two sides, tired of the ensuing guerrilla warfare, came to a conference table in Boston in February 1880. Santa Fe voluntarily gave up its lease with Rio Grande and the rights to the Royal Gorge Canyon. In essence, the Santa Fe was allowed to continue its transcontinental conquest while the Denver & Rio Grande was allowed to expand locally in Colorado.

Yet it was a hollow victory for Palmer. The D&RG remained a troubled line for years to come, undergoing three bankruptcies in the ensuing years.

California, Here We Come

During this era of conflict, the ATSF decided to continue westward from Santa Fe to California. There was little farming population in New Mexico from which the Santa Fe could draw business and revenue, and it badly needed the business to be found in the Golden State.

Santa Fe purchased a half interest in a charter owned by the St Louis & San Francisco Railway (the 'Frisco'), permitting the ATSF to forge into California. The Santa Fe, however, did not know that Jay Gould and CP Huntington possessed controlling interest in the Frisco line.

These two investors did not want the Santa Fe to cross the Colorado River into California where it could compete with the SP and the Texas & Pacific. But the Santa Fe held its ground, working a deal to serve southern California. Later, the

Santa Fe aquired the Chicago, Cincinnati & St Louis Railway which owned track between Chicago and the Mississippi River. From there it constructed a line across the river to connect with its own lines in Kansas. The two acquisitions gave the Santa Fe more than 7000 miles of track, with operations from the Great Lakes to the Gulf of Mexico and the west coast.

But expansion did not ensure its success. In the 1890s the railroad, subjected to the same economic pressures that were bankrupting competing lines, fell into receivership. Yet bankruptcy was but a temporary low point in the history of the line, and better times were ahead. After his success in the Colorado railroad wars, Strong became president and began expanding the Santa Fe system from 2000 miles to 7000 miles—with tracks running from California to both the Gulf of Mexico and the Great Lakes.

Strong added rolling stock and spent money to improve trackage, increasing equipment from 5530 units in 1880 to 32,293 in 1895. He ordered new, heavier steel tracks on the main lines, replacing old ties with treated ones.

With new steel track and improved rolling stock came larger locomotives. Like other railroads, the Santa Fe had long favored 4–4–0s, but in the 1880s the Santa Fe began using larger locomotives, 2–6–0s and 4–6–0s from the Baldwin Locomotive Works and Brooks Locomotive Works, to pull trains of increasing length and load.

In the late 1880s, because of reduced rates and increased interest payments on company debt, the ATSF suffered declines in revenues and earnings. Despite the fact that Strong was

buying more locomotives and rolling stock each year, shortages continued to plague the system and the slide continued into the early 1890s.

In 1896, Edward Ripley took over as president of the system and engineered the Santa Fe out of receivership. During his 24 years in control, Ripley expanded trackage to more than 11,000 miles and laid the foundations for the renaissance of company health that continues today.

Ripley, who spent time working on various railroads before coming to the Santa Fe, brought with him a reputation for honesty, integrity and leadership. He was responsible for eventually transforming the Santa Fe into one of the most successful railroads in modern America.

The Santa Fe had already proven to be a formidable competitor in southern California when, at the request of farmers and growers in California's Central Valley, Ripley brought the Santa Fe to San Francisco to counter the Southern Pacific's economic stranglehold on freight rates and traffic in northern California.

The SP was charging extremely high local rates to move goods and products from the Central Valley to San Francisco and it charged even higher rates on transcontinental routes. In fact, only competition from independent steamship lines had prevented the SP's Huntington from charging more.

Fed up, shippers in San Francisco organized the San Francisco Traffic Association to fight the so-called 'Octopus,' enlisting Ripley and the Santa Fe to assist. They proposed con-

Opposite: **A couple of coal burners assist** *El Capitan* **on Raton Pass.** *Above:* **A replica of the Coyote Special.** *Below:* **The first** *California Limited.*

Above: Fred Harvey, railroad restauranteur *par excellence. At right:* The Harvey House restaurant in Hutchinson Kansas, photographed in 1926.

structing an independent railway from Stockton through the San Joaquin Valley to San Francisco.

California sugar magnate Claus Spreckles spearheaded the effort, contributing enough money to encourage other investors to participate. Sacramento lawmakers helped by introducing a state charter for the San Francisco and San Joaquin Valley Railroad, which became known as 'The People's Railroad.' The ATSF purchased controlling interest in the company and continues to operate on the track today.

Fred Harvey

For those who traveled the Santa Fe's elite passenger trains, the name Fred Harvey conjured up great gastronomic memories. Harvey single-handedly transformed the business of serving food to rail travelers into an art—an art that has been lost with the advent of airline travel.

Yet in the 1870s, few travellers argued that the worst food in the United States was served at railroad depots. Dining cars were almost nonexistent, so the passengers had to disembark at depots along the way to gather a quick meal of rancid bacon, canned beans, eggs and biscuits. The biscuits were known as 'sinkers' because of their heavy soda content. Cold tea or bitter black coffee was also part of the menu. The engineer usually stopped the train for perhaps 10 minutes at lunch and at supper, while the conductor sent passengers scurrying to the depot restaurant.

The food was so bad that it became the focus of many jokes and gags by cartoonists and newspaper pundits. Even the railroad owners and their employees hated the situation. Train

crews suffered more because they were on the road all the time and were forced to exist on this food.

But Frederick Henry Harvey changed all that. He believed that quality and service at the lunch counter were as important as speed and safety aboard trains. Born in England, he had migrated to the United States when he was 15. He first entered the restaurant business in St Louis in 1856 when he was 21. Harvey perfected his cooking philosophy at several roadhouses in Kansas, where he succeeded in his business by serving good food. Then in 1876 he went to Santa Fe with his idea.

The superintendent of the Santa Fe agreed and gave Harvey permission to set up a restaurant in one of the company's stations. The Santa Fe put up the space, some materials and supplies, while Harvey put up his experience and ideas. The arrangement was sealed with a handshake.

Harvey took over one of the dining rooms at the Topeka station and transformed it with paint, new tablecloths, napkins and silver. He immediately started serving such good food that within a few months, train passengers clamored to get off the trains for a taste of Fred Harvey's food, and the Santa Fe Railroad decided to finance Harvey at other stations.

His next venture was the rundown dining room at Florence, Kansas—which he outfitted with elegant wood furniture and silver from England and with linen from Ireland. He hired

away the chef from the Palmer House Hotel in Chicago, telling him to serve the best food that money could buy. Soon the 'Florence House' became known far and wide as the place that served the best meals in Kansas.

In fact, Santa Fe travelers planned overnight stays at Florence just so they could sample the cuisine. It was curious, because the town of Florence had only 100 people. The Florence House was an idea whose time had come. By the time Fred Harvey died (in 1901) he had established 47 restaurants, 15 dining cars and 15 hotels in partnership with the Santa Fe.

Fred Harvey became an institution, and his restaurants became known for his 'Harvey Girls,' who became so famous in fact that a movie starring Judy Garland was made about their life and times. The girls were recruited from classified newspaper advertisements in midwestern and eastern newspapers. He sought 'Young women of good character, attractive and intelligent,' from 18 to 30 years of age to work for his firm. The women were required to live in dormitories where the nightly curfew was set at 10 pm.

Their standard uniforms consisted of black dresses with matching black shoes and hosiery, set off with white lace collars and black bows. They were instructed to wear their hair simply with a plain black bow. The pay was not extraordinary,

but benefits more than made up for the modest wages, which started at $17.50 per month and included room and board. Of course, they also got to keep the tips.

The women promised not to marry for one year, but many broke their promises and married earlier. Yet Harvey always congratulated those girls who managed to stay at work for more than 12 months without an engagement ring. Many of the waitresses married Santa Fe employees. Officials estimate that more than 5000 of them married railroad engineers, conductors or station agents, with a resulting 4000 babies who were named either Fred or Harvey.

Unlike modern chain restaurants where food was uniform, Harvey's restaurants took a different approach. His depot restaurants served passengers food that was readily available in the region. In California, for example, travelers were served fresh fruit and seafood, while in Chicago they got whitefish and corn.

With the invention of the refrigerator car, Harvey changed America's dining habits. When someone from Chicago got on a Santa Fe train, he found a menu featuring California fruit and specialties, while eastbound passengers were fed Kansas City steaks.

Santa Fe benefited from the food service through increased patronage, though it was never calculated how much money Santa Fe made or lost on its investment in the restaurants, hotels and rail dining cars. Harvey sometimes lost money, but never because of his service. He was guided by one principle: to serve the customers at any cost.

In fact, a story was told that one of his restaurants was losing $1000 a month. Soon the deficit was cut to $500 a month, but when Harvey investigated on one of his unscheduled survey trips he found that service had been trimmed—against his orders—so he fired the station manager. The $1000 monthly losses resumed, but no one seemed to care as long as the quality of service remained high.

Below left: These Harvey Girls were typical young ladies of the early 20th century. *Below:* The massive Harvey House in Dodge City, Kansas.

Below: Santa Fe's excellent luggage service at the height of the passenger era: when you got off the train, there it was. *Above:* The Santa Fe's *Grand Canyon* passes a freight on El Cajon Pass, where the main line crosses the Coastal Range. *At right:* A June 1951 Santa Fe ad.

Unlike the earlier days, when passengers were given 10 minutes to grab a meal, Harvey decreed that sufficient time for meals be granted to passengers at depot stops. He boasted that no passengers on the Santa Fe were ever forced to gulp down a meal or miss a train. Travelers at last had time to enjoy their food.

He served not only train crews and passengers, but local people as well. When he opened one of his popular restaurants in a new town on the western frontier, townspeople sometimes saw it as a threat to their local eateries. So, to keep the peace in such places, Santa Fe officials insisted that their station restaurants were open to serve the traveling public.

One of the reasons for ill feeling among townsfolk was Harvey's prices. He often charged less for a meal than the prevailing rates because, receiving supplies freight-free via the Santa Fe, his costs were lower, and most of his supplies and food were of better quality than that grown locally. This arrangement allowed his cooks to serve tastier, fresher and cheaper meals than the competing local restaurants could.

When Fred Harvey died his son took over and the restaurant chain continued to prosper. In World War II, Harvey served some 30 million meals in one year alone. However, the restaurants declined with the parallel decline of passenger service in the 1950s and early 1960s.

Passenger Trains

Santa Fe created a standard for passenger train service that was matched by few American railroads. For example, the New York Central's *Twentieth Century Limited*, a name that became synonymous with luxury and prestige, was equally matched by Santa Fe's *Super Chief*—the first all-diesel, all-Pullman streamliner in the United States.

The crystal Pleasure Dome of the new Super Chief—one of the many new features setting a New World Standard in Travel.

"Top of the Super - next to the stars !"

New Super Chief

You've seen dome cars on trains—but never before one like this!

In the dome lounge on the all-new Super Chief, your individual sofa seat turns so you can look ahead, look back or all around to view thrilling scenery by day. At night you can almost "reach up and pick a star."

Come and enjoy, too, the distinctive Turquoise Room—the only private dining room on rails—the lounges, Fred Harvey food, all-room and room-suite accommodations, Santa Fe hospitality all the way.

Ride the new *Super Chief*—any day you choose—between Chicago and Los Angeles. Just see your local ticket agent for reservations.

Santa Fe

Ride Great Trains through a Great Country

R. T. Anderson, General Passenger Traffic Manager, Santa Fe System Lines, Chicago 4, Illinois

The gracious way is Santa Fe

You're in the lap of luxury aboard the Santa Fe *Super Chief.* Gourmet Fred Harvey food. Impeccable service. Fun in the lavish lounges. Soft music. Superb scenery. VIP passenger list. If you want resort-style luxury, travel *Super Chief.*

Santa Fe

Super Chief

Daily between Chicago and Los Angeles
For reservations, contact any Santa Fe Traffic Office or Travel Agent

Introduced in 1937, *The Super Chief* sped between Chicago and Los Angeles in 39.5 hours, which was more than 14 hours faster than its steam predecessor, *The Chief. The Super Chief* became known for its luxury and food and, in the 1940s and 1950s, was the train for the rich and famous.

Santa Fe was not the first railroad to use diesels for passenger service, but it was the first to take advantage of diesel power plants for streamlined passenger service from the midwest to the west coast. The first prototype General Motors diesel engines were used to generate power for the Chevrolet assembly line at the Century of Progress exhibition in Chicago in 1933.

Although extremely experimental, diesels attracted the attention of the Burlington Railroad, which was seeking a revolutionary new train to attract passengers lost to the automobile. Burlington pursuaded GM to make one of the engines available for its new train. Despite reluctance on the part of GM, the engine and the experimental train proved successful and the age of the diesel locomotive was born.

The Super Chief

The original *Super Chief* featured two twin-diesel locomotives built by the Electromotive Corporation, a General Motors subsidiary at La Grange, Illinois. The locomotives, each rated at 3600 horsepower, were constructed in two units and were tested in different terrain and conditions before they were delivered to the Santa Fe. When the twin locomotives were put to the test hauling a nine-car Pullman, they broke the record set in 1905 by the Santa Fe steam locomotive, the *Coyote Special.*

With the test completed, the results were conclusive—diesel locomotives were here to stay. All that was needed was a sturdier trackbed to support the high-flyer passenger train. Santa Fe spent $4 million improving the tracks and the roadbed between Los Angeles and Chicago before putting *The Super Chief* into day-to-day service.

The diesel engines of the two locomotives proved they were better than steam engines and could operate at higher speeds for longer distances without expensive water stops along the way. Such water stops were required by steam locomotives, especially in desert climates.

The entire train was constructed of stainless steel, with sleepers from the Pullman Company and with club, baggage, dining and lounge cars constructed by the Budd Company. The cars were named after the Indian pueblos: Isleta, Laguna, Acoma, Cochiti, Oraibi, Taos and Navajo. With a full passenger manifest, the train carried 104 people, not including the train crew and eight postal clerks.

The second *Super Chief* unit also featured nine cars, giving Santa Fe twice-a-week service between Chicago and the west coast. In the later 1930s, five-car trains were added to the streamliner service, giving Santa Fe 13 streamliners, which was more than any other railroad in the US.

The first diesels did not have quite the charm of the Santa Fe's *De Luxe,* a six-car passenger steam train that carried 70 passengers on its first run in 1911. This train featured two drawing room cars, an observation car, a dining car and a club car as well as showers, tub baths, electric hair-styling irons and a fiction library. Its crew consisted of a ladies' maid, a barber, a manicurist and a hairdresser. The extra fare to take advantage of

Above left: A December 1960 *Super Chief* advertisement. *At right:* Two nine year old boys size up a retired Santa Fe steam loco in the age of diesels.

this service was $25, and the trip took 63 hours to make the 2267-mile run.

Many railroads, including the Santa Fe, prided themselves on their dining car service—even though most dining cars lost money. They were operated as loss leaders, with the expectation that excellent food and service would draw passengers from competing lines. The theory worked to the advantage of the Santa Fe and Fred Harvey. Santa Fe made money on its passenger service with reliable service and good food.

For a time, Santa Fe tried to cooperate with the coming of air travel. In 1929, the railroad pioneered cross-country service via the New York Central and Universal Air Lines. Passengers left New York for Cleveland, where they boarded an airplane that flew to Kansas City. There they boarded a train bound for Los Angeles, a trip which took three nights and two days. The service continued long enough for better passenger planes to come into service, thus rendering the train connections obsolete.

Throughout the early days of railroading, few improvements were made to dining cars. George Pullman had taken out the original patents in 1865 for cars in which passengers could sit and eat. But it was not until 1925 that the Santa Fe put its own design in service in hopes of creating an advantage over its rail competitors. A two-car set placed at the front of passenger trains included a diner and club lounger, with bath, barber shop and soda fountain, and held 42 customers in the diner alone. The trains also featured sleeping and shower facilities for the crew.

When the diesel proved its value in passenger service, Santa Fe officials set about replacing its freight service fleet of steam locomotives. The Electromotive Corporation delivered a 5400-horsepower engine to the railroad in 1938 nicknamed *The Jeep* and given the number 100. *The Jeep* hauled its first train of 68

Opposite: The Super Chief winds through Apache Canyon, near Lamy, New Mexico. Above: Santa Fe Number 2649 is an updated version of a 1945-era loco like Number 223, at left. Both are shown at Santa Fe's shops in Cleburn, Texas, in 1970. Below: Santa Fe's vintage Number 3460, the Blue Goose.

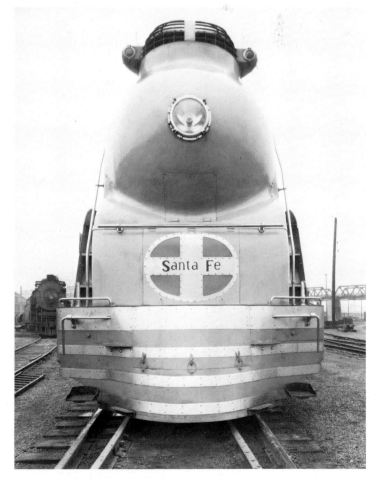

freight cars from Kansas City to Los Angeles under regular operating conditions, and proved that it could haul more freight cars up a grade at a higher speed than any steam locomotive in service at the time. No 100 trimmed the time it took a freight train to traverse the distance from Chigago to Los Angeles from six to four days and then three days. In 1938, hauling a train from the Great Lakes to the west coast by steam required nine engines and a total of 35 stops for fuel and water. No 100, on the other hand, required just five stops.

Diesel power plants were unique. Instead of one big steam plant, each diesel unit held four 900-horsepower diesel motors which generated current to drive eight traction motors directly connected to the truck axles. If problems developed in one of the two diesel units, the other unit would continue to produce power, allowing the diesels to run continuously for long periods without major delays. On the other hand, if steam engines experienced trouble they were forced to shut down, and sometimes entire trains had to be halted until repairs could be made.

In addition, steam locomotives were available for just one-third of their operating lives, with the other two-thirds spent in repairs (although many roundhouse mechanics managed to keep some steam locomotives operating 60 percent of the time). Diesels, however, could be in service 95 percent of the time.

Soon after the introduction of diesels in the 1930s, the fastest runs in the United States for both freight and passenger service were achieved by the new locomotives, and the days of steam were numbered. By 1943 two Santa Fe operating divisions were completely diesel, and by 1959 the last steam locomotives had been retired from the fleet.

The Santa Fe had established its reputation for fast, reliable and comfortable passenger service long before the arrival of *The Super Chief*. For example, Ripley was given credit for establishing *The California Limited*—for years, one of the best known trains form the midwest to the west coast. It was an all-Pullman train, and all passengers had to purchase tickets. No free passes were allowed, not even for Ripley. Whenever he rode the train, he presented his ticket to the conductor just like the other passengers.

The Limited was extremely popular in the summer months when people were headed to and from California. Each day as many as seven trains, each containing 11 sleeping cars filled with passengers, left Dearborn Station near Chicago or Union Station in Los Angeles within a half hour of each other. At one point, no fewer than 45 trains operated between the two cities—a record never broken.

The 45 trains—22 eastbound and 23 westbound—operated over the tracks simultaneously. During the three-day run, each train used a minimum of 15 locomotives with 15 train crews. For more than 10 years, *The California Limited* was the grandest and most popular train in the world.

Experiments with Freight Locomotives

While the Santa Fe was guarding its reputation for passenger service, it was also upgrading the size and speed of its freight locomotives. By 1911, the Santa Fe shops had built some of the largest steam locomotives ever constructed.

In one case, two engines were constructed from four older locomotive 2–8–0s. These engines, 2–8–8–0 *Mallets*, were followed by the construction of two big engines constructed for

This is the way you **see people and places** on the Santa Fe

not this way

For enjoyable "ground-level" (close-up) views of the colorful Southwest between Chicago and California . . .
For quiet privacy. For a choice of wonderful Fred Harvey meals . . .
For room to roam around when you feel like stretching your legs . . .
Go Santa Fe *all the way!*
Remember, too, you board Santa Fe trains downtown—not out in the sticks. You leave on schedule in any weather, arrive safely, relaxed, refreshed.

Santa Fe

Ride great trains through a great country

R. T. Anderson, General Passenger Traffic Manager, Santa Fe System Lines, Chicago 4.

Opposite, above: A service since taken over by Amtrak, Santa Fe's *San Diegan* speeds along the San Clemente coast. *Opposite:* Santa Fe locomotives lined up historically, left to right—from steam to diesel. *Above:* A Santa Fe 'anti-aircraft' ad. *Overleaf:* Unveiled at a 1938 exhibition, these Santa Fe diesels were in revolutionary contrast to the then state-of-the art steam locomotive, the *Blue Goose*, second from left.

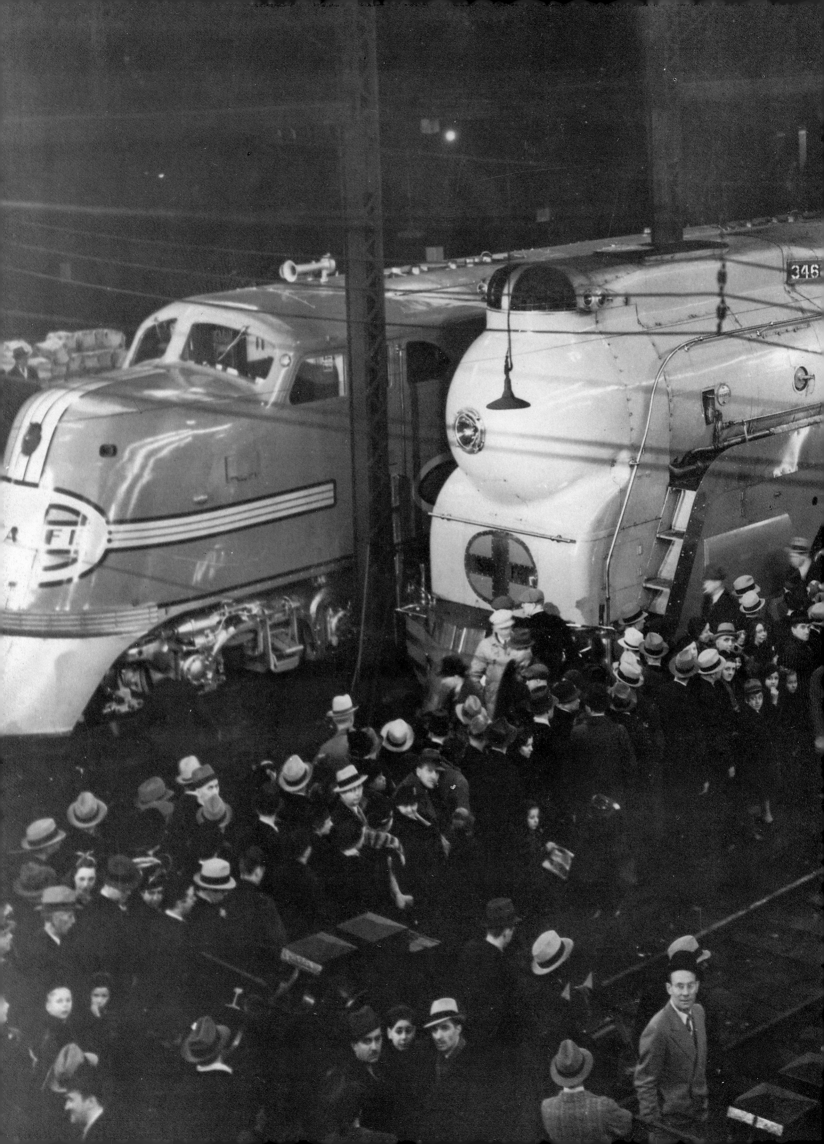

passenger service with a wheel arrangement of 4–4–6–0. They were used for six years, then rebuilt.

Baldwin also brought out two huge *Mallets* with a wheel arrangement of 2–8–8–2, which Santa Fe later reconstructed into four 2–8–2 types. The quest for size ended in 1911 when Santa Fe built 10 *Mallets* with a wheel arrangement of 2–10–10–2. They were the largest in the world but, despite their tractive power of 111,600 pounds, were unsuccessful and were later rebuilt into smaller 2–10–2 units.

Santa Fe designers wanted Baldwin to give the 'super locomotive' concept one more shot, with the construction of a quadruplex, double compound *Mallet* 2–8–8–8–8–2. The boiler was to have been flexible, with a joint in the middle, and with two cabs, one in front and one in back. It would have weighed more than 442 tons and would have had a tractive power of 220,000 pounds. But it was never built.

Setting a Record

The Santa Fe grew accustomed to setting speed records between its two major cities—Los Angeles and Chicago—long before *The Super Chiefs*. But the event that established the Santa Fe as one of the fastest lines came on 1 July 1905 when a man called 'Death Valley Scotty' (real name, Walter Scott) wrote out a check for $4500 so that he could reach Chicago in 46 hours.

Scotty, who reportedly had made his fortune in mining in California's Death Valley, was a colorful man who had worked

Above left and below right: Santa Fe quadruple header freights. Lower left: The SP and the Santa Fe on the Tehachapi Loop. Above: A Santa Fe boxcar.

at many things in his lifetime, even touring the world as a cowboy showman with the famous Indian scout, 'Buffalo Bill.'

Scotty had visited the station to ask if the Santa Fe could get him to Chicago in less than 50 hours. Railroad officials said they could, which set the stage for a dramatic run at the speed record.

After accepting his check, the Santa Fe told Scotty to show up with suitcase in hand the next day. When he returned, the railroad made appropriate plans for making an assault on the record, putting together a special train, *The Coyote Special*, and bringing it to Los Angeles' La Grande Station.

The train consisted of a Pullman-observation car, a diner and a baggage car, all pulled by a 2–6–0 *Baldwin*. With Scotty and his party on board, and the press there to report on the progress of the trip, the *Coyote Special* left promptly at 1 pm with a crowd of well wishers there to see them off.

Fast engine changes were made along the way, with 80 seconds considered slow, and the train reached speeds of up to 106 miles per hour during the trip. The ride was front-page news all across the country, with Associated Press journalist Charles E Van Loan filing dispatches as the train sped along.

Scotty and the other members of his party dined on caviar sandwiches, boiled squab and porterhouse steak, with fresh ice cream as dessert. Of course, champagne flowed throughout the trip.

A few miles before the end of each division change, Scotty would scramble over the coal tender into the crew compartment to hand $20 gold pieces to the engineer, fireman and division superintendent.

The Coyote Special pulled into Chicago at 11:54 am on July 12—just under 44 hours traveling time from Los Angeles.

Evolution of the Santa Fe Logo

| 1888-1895 | 1895-1896 | 1896-1899 | 1899-1901 | 1901-Present |

Nineteen engines and eight different crews had been used on the journey—a record that stood for many years until the arrival of the Santa Fe diesel locomotive, *The Super Chief.*

Santa Fe Today

In the 1980s the Santa Fe has emerged as one of America's most successful railroads. When the scheduled merger with the Southern Pacific Transportation Company is completed, the Santa Fe will emerge as—in terms of trackage—the nation's second largest railroad behind the Burlington Northern.

But the Santa Fe, like most railroads, is facing problems associated with increased competition. Officials announced in late 1986 that in coming years they plan to sell or abandon 3100 miles of track and dispose of nearly 8000 cars and 200 locomotives. In addition, more than 4100 employees are expected to lose their jobs through layoffs, retirement and ordinary attrition.

The Santa Fe merger with the Southern Pacific system is an attempt to become more competitive by streamlining operations. Despite financial setbacks, the ATSF remains one of the most innovative systems in the United States. More than 8900 miles of its mainline track is continuous-weld rail, and its freight trains speed along with high-tech signaling, scheduling and dispatching.

Santa Fe mechanical engineers designed and built the first tri-level auto car, which revolutionized the shipping of automobiles by rail. The company also was the first to attract traffic away from the Panama Canal by introducing the 'land bridge' to save shippers time. It now uses intermodal stack trains to move goods form west coast ports to midwest markets.

The Santa Fe story is entwined with the history of the Wild West, but the full story has yet to be told. The romantic days of the Santa Fe steam locomotives and high-speed luxury passenger trains have disappeared, but efficient, service-oriented freight service is expected to thrive in the years ahead.

Below: **A Santa Fe-Southern Pacific triple header hauls the goods near Buenos, Texas. When the planned merger goes through, these two lines will continue their current efficiency in handling freight shipments. The Santa Fe's innovations in rolling stock and roadbed will keep the line well alive.**

The Atchison, Topeka & Santa Fe

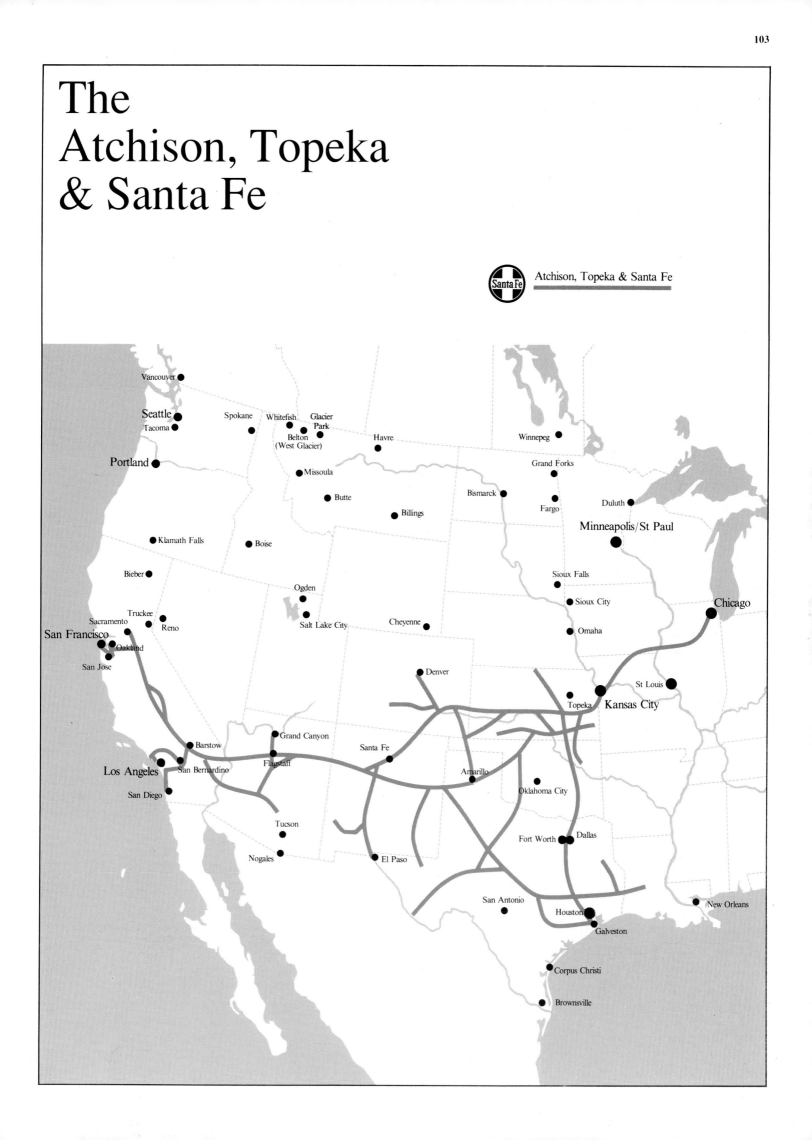

Atchison, Topeka & Santa Fe

BURLINGTON NORTHERN

The Burlington Empire

The story of the Burlington Northern Railroad is the story of the building of a great transportation empire from the midwest to the Pacific northwest. It is also the story of one of the greatest railroad empire builders—James J Hill.

Today the St Paul, Minnesota-based Burlington Northern, which hauls coal, grain and forest products as well as other manufactured products and goods, is the second largest railroad in the United States and features the longest rail network in the nation, its track spanning more than 29,200 miles in 25 states and two Canadian provinces.

The BN runs from the west coast across the Rockies to the Great Lakes and down to the eastern coast of Mexico. It operates 3000 locomotives and 130,000 freight cars and is the largest rail system operating in North America today. The CSX system is larger, on paper, but since some of its operating companies have more autonomy, they are considered independent companies.

The BN represents the merger of five major lines, with the history of its oldest line stretching as far back as 1850. The companies were the Chicago, Burlington & Quincy Railroad, the Great Northern Railway, the Northern Pacific Railway and the Spokane, Portland & Seattle Railway. The St Louis & San Francisco Railway (The Frisco) was added a decade later, while the Colorado & Southern Railway Company and the Denver Railway Company were added in 1981.

Great Northern

When the Great Northern Railway mainline reached the Pacific Ocean in 1893, one of the great ambitions of James Hill had been achieved. Hill, a Canadian born immigrant who later received US citizenship, had long dreamed of building a transcontinental railroad across the United States along the Canadian border. When he achieved his goal, he brought to the Pacific Northwest the benefits of a nationwide railroad system.

Hill was one of the great renaissance men of the 19th century and one of the more controversial of America's railroad barons. Always occupied with the building of his transportation empire, he sometimes took the time for other interests such as the intricacies of international trade and economics. But railroading remained his main passion and his life-long pursuit. 'Most people who have really lived' he said, 'have had, in some shape, their great adventure. The railway is mine.' In 1915, at the Panama–Pacific Exposition in San Francisco, the state of Minnesota named Hill as its 'greatest living citizen.'

Hill could be generous or vindictive, depending on his mood. He relocated one of his railroad stations more than a mile away from the center of a small town because the mayor

Opposite: A Great Northern diesel freight. The Great Northern was/is an important part of the Burlington Northern. *Below:* A retired BN caboose.

complained of the all-night switching at the station which sat at the center of town—and Hill didn't like the complaints.

Nevertheless, Hill could be a man of great imagination and patience. He conceived big ideas—like building a rail line from St Paul to Puget Sound—then spent years working on them. He looked to the future, projecting his ideas, then advancing to achieve them, an ability that enabled him to overcome the skepticism of those who said he could not reach the Pacific Coast with a railroad (especially without the advantage of the large land grants used to underwrite the construction of the Central Pacific and Union Pacific).

He was as shrewd as his peers and he fought vigorously with them to maintain control of his properties. When 'robber

At left: The somewhat egotistical, sometimes unscrupulous but very canny railroad baron James Hill. He was blind in one eye, but not blind to the possibilities of his, and other, railroads. *Below:* This Great Northern 4–4–0 paused atop Two Medicine Bridge, at Marias Pass near the Continental Divide.

baron' E H Harriman attempted to wrest control of Hill's railroad properties—the Burlington, the Northern Pacific and the Great Northern—Hill outmaneuvered Harriman by creating a joint system of ownership for them (although it was later dissolved by the US Supreme Court).

Great Northern's predecessor (it wouldn't become known as the Great Northern until 1890) originated in 1857 when the Minnesota legislature granted a charter to the Minnesota & Pacific Railroad Company to construct track in the direction of the Pacific Ocean. When the railroad went bankrupt a few years later, and its 60 miles of track and other assets were put under court jurisdiction, the St Paul & Pacific Railroad purchased the Minnesota & Pacific. However, it too fell into

bankruptcy in the Panic of 1873, along with dozens of other railroads.

For five years—from 1873 to 1878—the St Paul remained in receivership, partly the result of grasshoppers, which devoured everything and anything in their path throughout the region, and partly the result of poor economic conditions. The grasshoppers were so thick that even the heavy, eight-wheeled steam locomotives were slowed, then stopped, by the pests because they could not achieve traction on the rails. When the grasshoppers slowed the trains, they also slowed business.

Knowing the plague would not last forever, Hill persuaded three partners to join him in purchasing the St Paul & Pacific from the clutches of rival Northern Pacific. Two of the men,

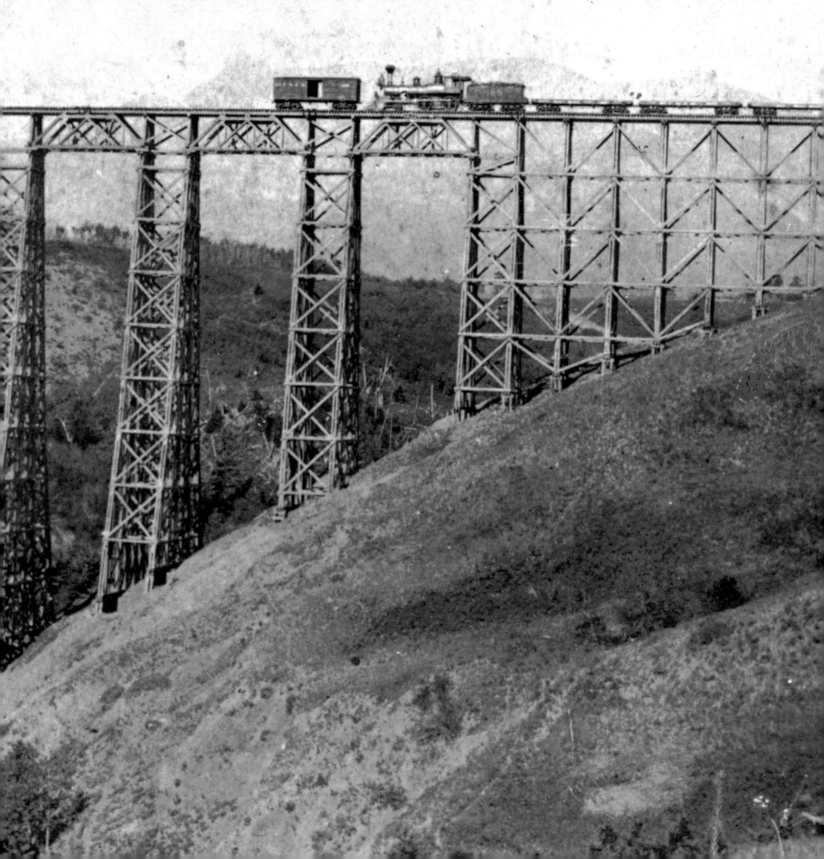

Above: This St Paul & Pacific 4–4–0 was the first locomotive in use on that road: having arrived at St Paul on a river barge in 1861, it became the grandpappy of Great Northern motive power. *Below:* An 1867 photo of a portage railroad's boat terminal and train on the US side of the Columbia River—the Great Northern would eventually cross to Canada here. *Below right:* The Northern Pacific's *Minnetonka* construction locomotive, built in 1870.

George Stephen, president of the Bank of Montreal, and Donald A Smith, chief commissioner of the Hudson Bay Company in British Columbia, became famous a few years later with the construction of the Canadian Pacific Railroad. The third, Norman W Kittson, became Hill's partner in the Red River Transportation Company.

They bought the St Paul & Pacific for about one-fifth of its actual value, snapping it up for $280,000 in cash and promissory notes. It was a shrewd purchase for Hill and his partners because the railroad was loaded with assets, despite its anemic cash flow and burdensome debts.

The St Paul possessed valuable federal and state charters and a land grant of five million acres. But since it was over-capitalized—owing $28 million in bonds to Dutch investors—it could not generate enough revenue to pay that debt. Hill and partners solved the cash-flow problem by waiting until the debit side of the balance sheet was wiped clean through foreclosure, then selling off the valuable land tracts and other assets for $13 million.

Hill had learned about the transportation business in 1865 when he first arrived in St Paul and worked as a clerk for a steamboat line on the Mississippi River. He had traveled to St Paul intending to team up with fur trappers and then to head west to seek his fortune; but he arrived too late in the season—the trappers had already departed—so he decided to stay in the city. He first tried to enlist in the Union Army during the Civil War, but was turned down because, as a young boy, he had lost the vision in one eye. Instead, Hill organized a group of volunteers. Otherwise, he spent most of his time working in a warehouse.

Hill eventually became an agent for the St Paul & Pacific; and when the St. Paul needed coal for its locomotives, he founded his own business—Hill, Griggs & Co—to sell the fuel as well as other goods. When the St Paul skidded into financial difficulties in 1873 and could not afford to buy large quantities of coal, Hill expanded his business, first into North Dakota and then into Canada. He established the Red River Transportation Line with Canadians Smith, Kittson and Stephen as partners. The company offered stage, riverboat and rail transportation between St Paul and Winnepeg.

Hill's ego expanded as his business acumen and success expanded, and he began to believe that when he was dead he would be hailed as one of the great business moguls of the times. His ego was evident in his living quarters—a grand sprawling castle in his beloved city of St Paul, Minnesota.

Under new ownership, the St Paul & Pacific continued its westward expansion—against the odds that it would be profitable. As track gangs laid down rails through northern forests and prairies, Hill beat the odds by using innovative programs to generate increased business for freight trains.

For example, Hill lured immigrants to the region for as little as $10 a person, as long as they agreed to settle along his railroad and work hard. Within a few years, thousands of immigrants, many of them from Scandinavian countries, were populating the region. 'Land without population,' Hill once said, 'is a wilderness. Population without land is a mob.'

For a while, he kept rates low, believing it more important to encourage increased traffic than to generate high profit margins. Later, when he had a monopoly on the transportation market, he raised rates. Some of the farmers did not like those rates, but they had no choice. Despite his exorbitant shipping charges, most farmers had to ship their crops on his railroad to the grain elevators and steamboats. 'After the grasshoppers,' they said, 'we had James Hill.'

Hill hired agricultural experts to show farmers in the region how to improve their crops and livestock. He was an early advocate of developing the mineral and natural resources of Minnesota and the surrounding region. Hill's incessant profit-

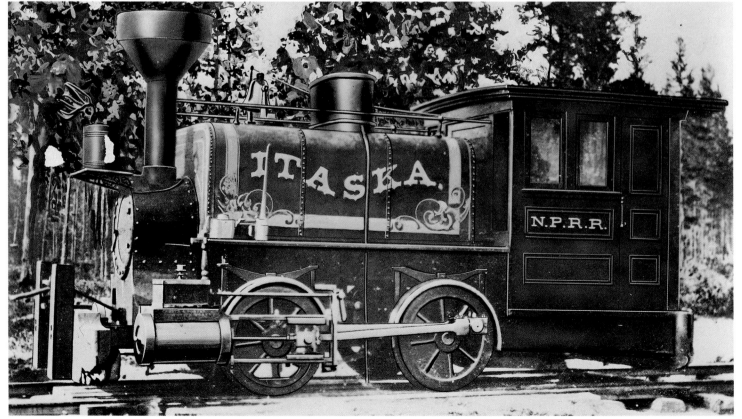

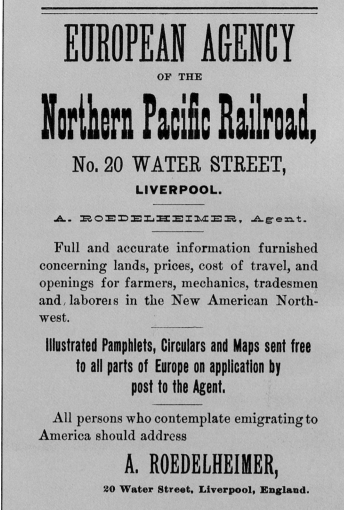

Above: One of Hill's ploys to create population for his rail routes. *Above left:* The NP loco *Minnetonka* (see also page 109) is shown here ready for exhibit at the Century of Progress Exhibition in Chicago, circa 1933. *Below left:* The NP's headlightless *Itaska,* with antlers and 'pusher' cowcatcher.

minded motivation enabled him to expand the St Paul and Pacific system rapidly, yet without the aid of subsidies given to underwrite other railroads.

He was continually seeking ways to expand and improve the business. In the 1880s and 1890s, for example, he wanted to know why export levels to the Orient through west coast ports were so low. When he found that price was the major consideration he started his own shipping company—the Great Northern Steamship Company—to increase the flow of American raw materials such as steel and lumber through west coast ports. His railroad benefitted from the increased traffic.

When he assumed control of the St Paul & Pacific, Hill drove the construction crews hard to expand to the north and west. To keep the line profitable and to achieve land grants, he had to build extensions called for under federal and state charters. So his crews put down as much as a mile and a half of track a day until the line reached the Canadian border.

He often held up construction until he had personally inspected progress on the railhead and given his final OK. It was the kind of attention to detail that would make Hill a legend. In 1887 the St Paul & Pacific set a record for track building—between April and mid-October, 545 miles of track were constructed between Minton, North Dakota and Great Falls, Montana.

At one point Hill employed 8000 men and 3300 horse teams. The crews, laboring in the unsettled wilderness of

North Dakota, Montana, Idaho and Washington, continued to set records despite unsettled weather conditions, roving bands of Indians and the logistics of the undertaking.

By 1890 Hill had adopted the Great Northern Railway Company as the new name for his railroad empire, a decision that better reflected the growth and strength of the railroad and the region it served—and the fact that he soon would have a line reaching all the way to the Pacific Ocean.

The final push of Great Northern's Pacific coast extension—which required spanning the Continental Divide at Marias Pass, one of the lowest passes through the Rockies—began the next summer at Havre, Montana. By the close of 1892, only a seven-mile gap in the Cascades in Washington state remained to be conquered. But this, too, proved to be no problem for Hill and his men. One year later, the crews punched a tunnel through the rugged Cascade Mountains, allowing the Great Northern to start transcontinental service, and Hill soon became known as 'the Empire Builder.'

Hill was not without his competitors or rivals—for instance, the competing Northern Pacific served similar territories. But Hill's attempts to merge the Great Northern with Henry Villard's Pacific Northern were twice ruled unconstitutional by the US Supreme Court. So the two railroad systems remained competitors until, in 1970, long after Hill had passed from the scene, the high court finally held that they could be merged into one system.

In 1916 James Hill died from an infection, and during his funeral, traffic on all of his railroads, steamship and other transportation lines was halted for five minutes. It was a fitting tribute to the man who, beginning life as a small-town clerk, had died as a legendary figure, the Empire Builder.

Northern Pacific

Despite his entrepreneurial spirit, Hill was not the first railroad pioneer to enter the mountains and valleys of the northern plains and the Pacific northwest. That distinction went to another man—one who, like Hill, was an immigrant from another land. But Henry Villard would not become a key player in the history of the Northern Pacific Railroad until well after construction had begun.

The Northern Pacific, which became the first northern transcontinental railroad, was created when President Abraham Lincoln signed legislation establishing the Northern Pacific Railroad Company (NP) with an eastern terminous on Lake Superior and a western terminus on Puget Sound in Washington state. The track followed the westward pioneering path blazed by Lewis and Clark.

Few other events in history had such impact on western railroading as the Lewis and Clark Expedition of 1804–1806. President Thomas Jefferson, realizing the significance of the territory west of the Mississippi, had signed the Louisiana Purchase in July 1803, bringing the region under the flag of the

Above left: Chinese laborers on the NP. *Below left:* A postcard of 1887 from Castle Rock, Washington, featuring NP trains. *Below:* A military guard, in case of Indian attack, and railborne worker's dormitories on the StPM&M. *Above:* A terribly rugged looking, but very efficient, StPM&M rail gang.

United States. Less than a month later, Captain Merriwether Lewis was on his way down the Ohio River to meet William Clark in Louisville. The two men later departed from St Louis on their historic expedition.

Few white men had made the journey across the plains and mountains of the western US, a trip which required traveling up the upper Missouri River, across the Rocky Mountains and down the Columbia River. But Lewis and Clark accomplished the arduous journey, returning two years later with carefully detailed notes and a diary describing the botany and wildlife

and the Indian customs and languages of the American west. It was an accomplishment that eventually spurred construction of a railroad into the region.

Today the main line of the Burlington Northern parallels the explorers' trail, running along the great Missouri, then along the Yellowstone, Gallatin and Jefferson rivers to Helena, Montana. The railroad crosses the Continental Divide, then picks up the trail again near the Snake River on the other side of the mountains. The tracks hug the Columbia River—the route used by the two great explorers—and passes through many cities along the way that were named by the explorer party.

The enabling legislation signed into law by Lincoln called for rights-of-way through public lands which extended for 200 feet on both sides of the tracks, as well as other land for sta-

At left: A seven car Great Northern passenger train, with two engines in front and one behind, zigzags up a Cascades switchback. Switchbacks enabled trains to climb steep slopes by dint of their angular approach. *Below:* A GN rotary snow plow, in the Rockies, circa 1911. *Above:* An 1880 photograph of GN track construction one mile west of Glacier National Park, Montana.

tions, repair buildings and other facilities. In addition, the act granted land to the railroad that could be sold to finance construction costs and capital purchases such as engines and rolling stock. But the lands were isolated and uninhabited and therefore worth very little until the railroad was actually constructed.

The NP was specifically forbidden to sell stocks or bonds to build the railroad, so the money had to be raised from other sources. Yet because of the immense size and the high cost involved, few investors were willing to put money into the project. Finally, Congress voted to allow the NP to issue bonds and then secure the bonds by a mortgage on its property—a decision that enabled the builders to raise the necessary capital to extend the railroad toward the Pacific Ocean.

The builders of the Northern Pacific relied on the early survey work of Edwin F Johnson, an eminent engineer who had written a book in the 1850s calling for a transcontinental line across the northern half of the US. He conducted extensive surveys up the Missouri River, then turned to Congress, seeking authorization for construction of a railroad along this route.

Formal groundbreaking ceremonies were held in 1870 near Duluth, Minnesota, where track gangs immediately began building westward. At the same time, other crews worked northward to connect Portland with Tacoma. Progress was interrupted by the Great Panic of 1873 when the Northern Pacific went bankrupt along with dozens of other US companies. When the railroad was rescued from receivership, it took five years to get the project under way again.

At left: In this 5 October 1911 photo, James J Hill drives the Golden Spike that completed his Oregon Trunk Railway. *Below:* This Northern Pacific 4–4–0 was decked out for the Golden Spike celebration in Gold Creek, Montana, which marked the completion of the NP's ambitious St Paul to Portland route.

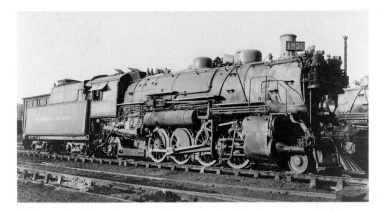

Above: A Northern Pacific 2–8–2 steam locomotive. *At bottom:* Built for the Great Northern in 1925, this gasoline-electric rail car eventually was sold used to the Montana Western, and now resides in the Mid-Continent Railway Museum. *At right:* A GN electric locomotive in Skykomish, Washington.

By 1879, Northern Pacific trackage had been constructed westward from the Dakota Territory in Montana, and by 1882 NP tracks reached what is now Livingston, Montana. But the company was now running into labor and material problems. It could not find enough laborers. As a consequence the NP turned to Chinese workers, just as the Central Pacific had done in the previous decade, and more than 15,000 Chinese were imported to relieve the general labor shortage. Meanwhile, rails, ties and spikes were imported from France and England to solve shortages in these materials.

General George Armstrong Custer and the famed 7th Cavalry were assigned to protect the Northern Pacific surveyors and construction crews in Montana Territory from marauding Indian bands. Custer attempted to bring them under his control and move them onto a reservation; but in one of the last and best known battles waged on the Great Plains—the battle of the Little Big Horn—Custer himself became a casualty.

However, the relentless advance of the white man into the region so overwhelmed the Indians, and progress on the Northern Pacific continued so well, that by the spring of 1883 only 300 miles separated the eastern from the western terminus of the Northern Pacific.

The large gap in the railroad system in this era was not bridged until Henry Villard became president of Northern Pacific. Once a penniless emigre from Germany, Villard studied law and journalism and eventually became a player on the stage of American history. He was first a reporter at the Lincoln-Douglas debates and at the Chicago Republican Convention where Abraham Lincoln was nominated for president. He later became a Civil War correspondent and even covered the gold rush on Pike's Peak in Colorado.

Villard had first been drawn to railroads when, as a young man he took a job as a crewman on a wood train of the Indiana

& Madison Railroad. Years later, during a visit to his native Germany, a group of European financiers convinced Villard to manage and protect their investments in American railroads. He agreed and was so successful that he eventually organized his own company, which purchased control of the Northern Pacific.

The Pacific leg and the midwestern leg of the Northern Pacific tracks were connected with great ceremony at Gold Creek, Montana in September 1883 in a lavish celebration that featured former President Ulysses S Grant and included distinguished guests from Germany, England and Scandinavia as well as 10 US senators and 20 members of Congress. Once the speeches were over, 300 men quickly put down the last thousand feet of track.

In the years that followed this celebration, the Northern Pacific prospered. It built connections to other railroads and branch lines which increased the political and economic power of the region. Less than seven years after the ceremonies at Gold Creek, the states of North Dakota, South Dakota, Montana and Washington had gained sufficient population to enter the Union—and to boost the fortunes and profitability of the Northern Pacific.

In 1901, the Northern Pacific and the Great Northern Railroads purchased controlling interest in the Chicago, Burlington & Quincy Railroad, giving the two lines access to

Chicago and the markets of the middlewest and south. Later, the two railroads jointly constructed and operated the Spokane, Portland & Seattle Railway, which became known as 'the Northwest's own Railway.'

During World War II, the Northern Pacific Railroad carried out a major rehabilitation program, reballasting and laying heavier rail on 2000 miles of its mainline track. More than 300 mainline curves were eliminated or reduced, while bridges and tunnels were replaced and new shops and freight houses were constructed.

In the postwar era the Northern Pacific introduced train radios, continuous-welded rail, centralized traffic control and other technological innovations. Like other rail lines, the steam engine fleet was modernized with diesel equipment in the 1940s and 1950s.

St Louis & San Francisco Railway Company

One of the most interesting facts about the St Louis & San Francisco Railway Company—better known as 'The Frisco'—is that it never reached its namesake on the California coast! The history of the Frisco is the history of a company that bat-

Above left: The GN *Empire Builder,* just before its maiden voyage. *Above:* A GN freight crosses the Skykomish River. *Below:* The sleek Burlington *Zephyr.*

tled against takeover attempts and changing circumstances, only to disappear.

In the year that gold was discovered at Sutter's Mill in the Sierra foothills of California, Missouri lawmakers chartered the Pacific Railroad of Missouri to run from St Louis to Kansas. They intended it to run through Indian territory westward along the 35th parallel to San Francisco, but it was not until 1855 that construction actually began on the route.

By the end of the Civil War, both the Missouri Pacific and its southwest branch were bankrupt. Part of the problem were the marauding bands of so-called 'Jayhawkers' and 'bushwackers' who terrorized the people of Missouri after the war. Considerable damage was wrought by these roving bands of armed men.

The two railroads were purchased by John C Fremont, the man known as 'The Pathfinder' and the son-in-law of Missouri Senator Thomas Hart Benton, who had been one of the driving forces behind the construction of a transcontinental railroad. He helped Fremont obtain a federal franchise and grant in the name of the Atlantic & Pacific Railroad.

The franchise allowed the A&P to extend a southwest branch to San Francisco along the 35th parallel. But Fremont was less successful in laying track than he had been in getting the franchise. In 1868, when Fremont failed to make the first payment on the loan, the railroad was sold to the state of Missouri.

During the next decade, track was extended west to the Indian territories, but in 1879 the Santa Fe Railway took control and used the A&P and its land grants to finance the construction of its own line from Albuquerque to California.

Numerous branch lines were constructed in the 1880s, but the dreams of the Missouri lawmakers were never realized. The railroad never reached the Pacific, but came to a stop just west of Tulsa, Oklahoma in the early 1880s.

In the mid-1890s the Frisco suffered bankruptcy along with the Santa Fe, and when it emerged from bankruptcy it was reorganized under a new name, the St Louis & San Francisco Railroad Company. The line was associated for a while with the Rock Island Line, which extended its tracks to the south. In 1980, the St Louis & San Francisco was merged with the Burlington system.

The Spokane, Portland & Seattle

The Spokane, Portland & Seattle Railway was organized in 1905 as a joint venture of the Northern Pacific and the Great Northern railroads to serve the farming regions of eastern Oregon and Washington, connecting Spokane with Portland. Its more than 1000 miles of track hugged the banks and shorelines of the Columbia and Snake rivers, for example, shadowing the north bank of those scenic rivers for nearly 300 of the 380 miles between Portland and Spokane.

The SP&S later laid tracks along the Deschutes River to Bend, Oregon, again following the river's curves and banks. Between Portland and the Pacific coast, the Columbia was used for another extension of the railroad, while yet another line was built from Portland south along the Willamette River and Tualatin River valleys to Eugene.

In the days of steam, less motive power was needed to operate the heavily laden trains along the river banks, which were natural settlements for a growing population. As a consequence, these natural corridors served as economically attractive ways to bridge the great mountain ranges of the Pacific northwest.

In the era before the private automobile, the SP&S offered as many as 50 daily passenger trains through the region, attracting hundreds of industrial plants to sites along its tracks. Meanwhile, construction of giant hydroelectric dams in the 1930s and 1950s brought new surges of industrial development and forced a relocation of the tracks along the north bank of the Columbia.

Bonneville Dam, completed in 1938, brought about the first major change of tracks. McNary Dam, completed in 1958, necessitated the second; and the Dallas Dam, completed in 1957, necessitated the third relocation.

In 1958, the Ice Harbor Dam on the Snake River, just east of its confluence with the Columbia, was completed, and when the John Dam was opened in 1966 near Cliffs, Washington, the SP&S crews had to move the tracks to higher grades above the slack-water pools behind the structures.

New rail, laid in an era of more advanced technology, won acclaim for the SP&S as one of the finest stretches of track in the nation, historians calling it the 'newest line in the west.' The railroad became part of Burlington Northern in 1970.

The Burlington Lines

The Burlington Lines were the oldest and largest of the company's predecessors. Beginning in 1850, workers from the Aurora Branch Railroad nailed second-hand strap iron to 12 miles of wooden rails to create the first rail system in Illinois.

Below, from left—5000hp electric, 5400hp four unit diesel and 2–8–8–2 steam. *Right:* The Burlington Northern's Guernsey, Wyoming fueling yard.

The rails had been purchased from the Buffalo & Niagara Falls Railroad at bargain prices, after the New York state legislature outlawed their use. With cars and locomotives borrowed from a competing line, Aurora's first train ran from Batavia to Turner Junction which is now within Chicago's city limits.

After Boston investors purchased the line in 1852, the Aurora Branch Railroad grew to 400 miles of track within 12 years. In 1864 it adopted the name of the Chicago, Burlington & Quincy Railroad Company, or the Burlington, and operated between Chicago and Aurora. At the end of the Civil War, it earned the distinction of operating the first train into Chicago's Union stock yards.

The Burlington prospered after the war under the direction of investor John Murray Forbes and Charles E Perkins, who hammered together a larger system from a collection of affiliates, tripling the size of the railroad between 1881 and 1901. Of the 204 railroads brought under control of the Burlington, two were outstanding properties—the Hannibal & St Joseph Railroad Company and the Burlington & Missouri River Railroad Company.

The Hannibal & St Joseph owed its existence to John M Clemens—later overshadowed by his son, Samuel W Clemens, or Mark Twain. In 1852 the elder Clemens helped to get construction on the railroad underway. By 1859 it was completed and carried mail across Missouri to the Pony Express stations. The company also introduced the first equipment to sort mail enroute. During the Civil War, the railroad was often raided by Confederate troops, and later by Jesse James and other train robbers.

Construction of the Hannibal & St Joseph established Kansas City as a major rail center and gateway, especially after the company built the first bridge over the Missouri River in 1869. The Burlington and the Hannibal & St Joseph railroads maintained close ties for many years until they were severed by Jay Gould and his New York allies, who used the Hannibal & St Joseph as a pawn for stock speculation and rate wars with other regional carriers. However, Perkins regained control of the line in 1883 and merged it into his growing Burlington system.

During the 1870s and 1880s the Burlington expanded west and north to Denver, St Louis and Rock Island, Illinois and westward to Billings, Montana. At the same time, the Burlington constructed or purchased branch lines in the farming regions of Illinois, Iowa, Missouri and Nebraska.

Transporting farm products was so critical to the financial success of the Burlington that within a few years it became known as a 'Granger Road.' Burlington employees worked closely with the farmers, advising them regarding what could be profitably planted in Missouri and introducing alfalfa as a commercial crop in Nebraska in 1875. Through seed and soil exhibits, poultry shows and livestock exhibitions, the Burlington built up business.

The Burlington also employed farmers at its repair shops during the winter months from harvest to planting season, a practice that enabled the farmers to stay profitable during the lean years.

Large land tracts in Missouri, Iowa and Nebraska were granted to the Burlington by Congress, enabling the company to hire as many as 250 agents in the east and to open offices in England, Scotland, Sweden and Germany. From 1870 to 1880, the railroad sold more than two million acres of land to 20,000 settlers from all over the world.

During this era the Burlington improved its fleet of steam locomotives and rolling stock, adding heavier rails and more

Above and below: Great Northern ads from the 1950s. *Opposite,* a ribbon of steel: A BN track crew replaces rails near Alliance, Nebraska.

powerful locomotives. In 1886 and 1887, inventor George Westinghouse perfected the air brake through tests made on the grade at West Burlington, Iowa. At the turn of the century, James J Hill gained control of Burlington stock through purchases made by his Great Northern and Northern Pacific railroad companies. Hill paid $200 per share for the stock, a high price at the time, but he considered it well worth it. He wanted to reach eastern markets beyond Minneapolis, and the Burlington provided that extension.

Hill understood that the great market centers of the midwest—such as Kansas City, St Joseph, Omaha, Chicago and St Louis—were critical to the growth and profits of his Pacific Northwest transportation empire. With the Burlington, he made money by importing goods from the Orient and carrying timber from the Pacific northwest in exchange for coal, minerals, livestock and other products from Texas and Colorado.

Still dissatisfied, Hill wanted to extend rail connections as far south as the Gulf of Mexico, so he purchased the Colorado & Southern and the Fort Worth & Denver railroads, which provided routes from Cheyenne and Denver to Fort Worth, Dallas and the port cities of Houston and Galveston. With a link from Cheyenne to Billings, Montana, Hill finally obtained a coast-to-coast line all the way from Puget Sound to the Gulf of Mexico—right across the heartland of America.

However, with the Panama Canal Act of 1914, which forbade Hill's lines from carrying materials between the Gulf of Mexico and the Pacific Ocean, Congress blocked his plans and his dream of a transcontinental railroad empire. The act had put a stop to his grand strategy of creating a land bridge between the Gulf and the Pacific.

Below: The GN mountain goat is emblematic of Glacier National Park, part of the GN's 'turf.' *Inset, opposite:* GN and NP routes are here differentiated.

Pioneering Passenger Diesels

At the end of the age of steam, the Burlington was widely known for its role in introducing the diesel locomotive to American railroads. In May 1934, the Burlington staged one of the most publicized transportation events of the decade when its Pioneer Zephyr—the nation's first diesel-powered, streamlined passenger train—broke a record for the 1000-mile run between Denver and Chicago. The trip firmly established the value and efficiency of the diesel locomotive for both passenger and freight use. Within the span of a few years after that trip, virtually every railroad in the nation had replaced their old steam units with diesels.

During the record-breaking trip, radio stations broadcast news bulletins as the train sped past villages and cities. In Chicago, a large crowd of curious onlookers gathered at the station to greet the historic train on its arrival. The Burlington president later reported to his board of directors that the trip had cost just $14.64 in diesel fuel, while reaching a speed of 112.5 miles per hour.

With the success of the Zephyr the Burlington began converting its system to diesel, including its commuter trains in and around Chicago. The first freight diesels were purchased in 1944, and by the early 1950s more than 95 percent of Burlington's power was diesel.

In the first half of the 20th century the Burlington also set records as one of the premier passenger carriers, introducing in 1945 the first vista-dome car, and introducing in 1950 the first double-deck, stainless steel, air-conditioned suburban passenger cars. Those same cars continue to operate today on suburban commuter trains in Chicago and on the San Francisco peninsula.

Evolution of the Great Northern Logo

1895-1912

1912-1921

1921

1921-1936

1921-1936

1936-1967

1967-1970

The Burlington Northern

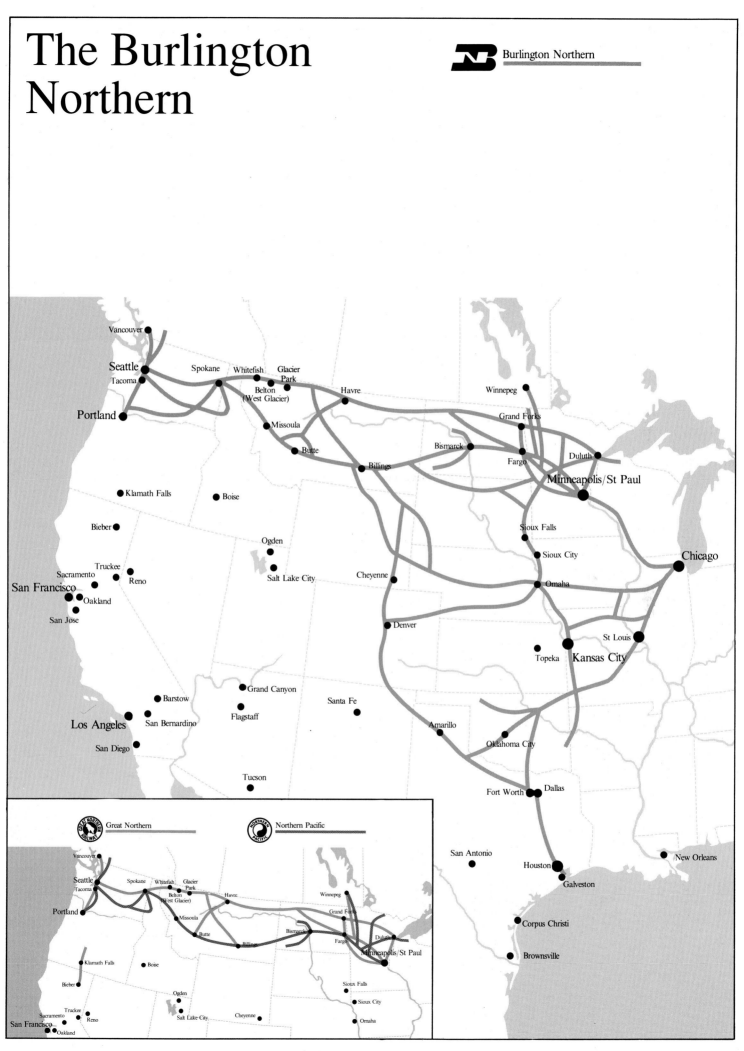

Burlington Northern

Great Northern

Northern Pacific

CANADIAN PACIFIC

A Diversified Empire

For more than a century, CP Rail was called the Canadian Pacific Railway, and it remains today the railroad that helped to settle the Canadian west in the second half of the last century. With its long hauls and vast resource base, CP Rail has long been a prosperous railroad.

Today the parent company—known as Canadian Pacific Limited and *Canadien Pacifique Limitee*—is a diversified company with assets in excess of more than $8 billion in land, sea and air transportation, as well as investments and holdings in telecommunications, natural resources, hotels and real estate and financial service.

CP Rail operates trains over more than 21,500 miles of track in Canada—a distance slightly less than the circumference of the Earth. The company also operates another 4600 miles in the United States. In the early 1980s, CP Rail deployed more than 1225 diesel locomotives and 62,000 freight cars and employed more than 29,000 workers.

The CP Rail system features one of the longest tunnels in North America—the Connaught Tunnel in British Columbia which is five miles, 117 feet long—and operates over the longest and highest bridge in Canada—the Lethbridge Viaduct in Alberta which is 5328 feet long and 314 feet high.

While the rail arm of this gigantic corporation is still known as the Canadian Pacific or CP Rail, other subsidiaries have different corporate designations, such as CP Air, CP Ships, CP Transport, CP Express and CP Hotels. The heaviest concentration of rail traffic on the system is between Vancouver and Calgary, particularly between Beavermouth and Revelstoke where more than 36 million tons of coal are carried in CP Rail coal trains.

The history of CP Rail began with the St Andres and Quebec Railroad, chartered in March 1836, and its oldest line in the United States, the Connecticut & Passumpsic River, chartered in October 1843.

Opposite: A distinctively red and white Canadian Pacific freight makes the grade near Revelstoke, British Columbia. *Below:* One example of CP subsidiary housekeeping exellence is this, the Chateau Lake Louise, in Alberta—just one of the luxurious hotels availed to the public by CP Hotels.

Between Two Coasts

The story of the Canadian Pacific began with trapper Alexander Mackenzie and other great fur traders who ventured to rugged western Canada in the last half of the 18th century and the first decades of the 19th. Mackenzie and his partners established small but important settlements along the west coast of Canada, and by the 1830s Canadians both in and out of government began to suggest a rail connection between Canada's Atlantic and Pacific coasts which would use the trappers' villages as wayside stops.

By this time, railway travel was an accepted practice in the eastern half of Canada—the world's second-largest nation—but it took almost 30 years to convince the British Dominion government to undertake the project. With the sale of the Hudson's Bay Company by the British to the Canadian British Dominion government in 1869, the officials finally gave serious consideration to a transcontinental railroad.

The government was already aware of the importance of such a transcontinental line. In that same year, the Central Pacific and Union Pacific railroads met at Promontory, Utah, where the golden spike hammered into the ground symbolized the unification of the eastern and western United States.

Settlers had petitioned the Canadian provincial government for a rail connection as early as 1863, and when a delegation from British Columbia discussed joining the confederation, they demanded a rail connection as one requirement.

In the final agreement admitting British Columbia to the Dominion, a clause was included calling for construction of a railroad within two years—that would be completed within 10 years of the starting date. The government decided to undertake responsibility for the project and committed itself to building more than 2600 miles of track across mountains, thick forests and open prairies.

Before track could be laid, surveys were needed, and the government chose Stanford Fleming to find a suitable route and complete detailed survey maps. Fleming, who had earlier worked on the Intercolonial railroad system, set out with a small party from Toronto in July 1872 and proceeded west by

way of Fort Garry (now known as Winnipeg). He and his men continued westward from Edmonton, trudging through Yellowhead Pass in the Rockies to Kamloops on the Thompson River before stopping for the winter.

Fleming resumed surveys the next spring, but the full task took six years, required hundreds of men and cost the Dominion more than $4 million. Fleming himself covered 46,000 miles of possible routes across the North American continent.

Fleming realized the immense challenges involved in building a railroad through sparsely settled wilderness. Supplies for his survey teams had to be shipped from 3000 miles away, while his men had to deal with raging forest fires and turbulent, churning rivers. More than a half-dozen men died in fires and another dozen drowned.

Fleming recommended a route running north of Lake Superior across the prairie to Edmonton and Yellowhead Pass. Once through the mountains, he recommended that the tracks parallel the Thompson River to Burrard Inlet, where the city of Vancouver is located today.

But government officials who studied the survey maps vetoed Fleming's recommendations and decided to build farther south—and closer to the United States. They did not want to lose business to the US railroads which were already proliferating in the region along the border. Later, other Canadian lines were constructed along the routes Fleming had recommended.

Crews were ordered to work in two directions—eastward from the west coast and westward from the east coast—until they met. Westward construction began in 1875, running west from Fort William.

Five years later, the section between Fort William and Selkirk on the Red River was completed about 16 miles south of present day Winnipeg. Westward progress halted temporarily while a rail line was driven south across the US border to St Vincent, Minnesota where connections were made with the Saint Paul & Pacific Railroad.

This diversion opened up the Canadian prairie west of the Red River, enabling Canadians to travel downriver in the

Above left: The Canadian Pacific Station at Lethbridge, Alberta, in 1899. Note the passengers' belongings—bicycle, cot and trunk—at the near end of the station house. *Above:* An early Canadian Pacific construction gang poses with their steam shovel. *Below:* Shown here as it existed on the original Canadian transcontinental railway, Mountain Creek Bridge—on the eastern slope of the Selkirks—was 164 feet high and 1086 feet long.

Chief commissioner of the Hudson's Bay Company Donald Smith *(above)* envisioned a grand role for the Canadian Pacific in Canada's future. William Cornelius Van Horne *(above right)* was the chief builder of the Canadian Pacific. *Facing page:* Donald Smith drives home a thrifty plain iron spike to seal the completion of the Canadian Pacific's transcontinental route.

Below: Flags and evergreens festoon the locomotive pulling Canada's first transcontinental train as it arrives in Port Arthur, Ontario in June 1886.

Above: The arrival of the first train in Port Moody, BC. *Below:* A Canadian Pacific work crew in the lower Fraser Valley in 1883. *Above opposite:* These men were building a retaining wall at Rogers Pass. *Below opposite:* Buffalo bones being loaded on a CP boxcar, circa 1880.

summertime to make connections with US trains going to the west coast. But by 1880, work on the main transcontinental line restarted, with eastern crews bridging the Red River in the east and other crews starting work in British Columbia. By the end of the year, more than 100 miles had been constructed west of the river and east of the inlet in more rugged and isolated terrain.

Progress continued despite arguments between the liberals and conservatives in Parliament as to whether the Canadian Pacific should be constructed privately or with government funds. Many did not believe that the government should shoulder the cost of construction alone. They argued that private enterprise should be involved. Fleming disagreed, but had no influence in the deliberations. When the liberals won a majority in 1882, political pressure forced Fleming to resign from office.

Work lagged while the government continued to look for private financing, but few investors in North America, especially in capital-poor Canada, showed an interest in completing the project. Finally, private investors from England offered to complete the Canadian Pacific in exchange for a grant of $25 million and 25 million acres of land, plus rights to certain rail lines already constructed. The Dominion government, anxious to complete the work, accepted this proposal.

The subsidies were to be paid in installments for each 20 miles of track completed, and the land was to be granted in alternate sections—just as had been done to spur financing and complete the transcontinental line in the United States.

The land for shops, yards and buildings would be given free by the government, while all construction material would be imported free of duties and taxes. Even the land grants were to be tax free for 20 years. The company was also permitted to float bonds of $25 million, using forest lands as security, before the line was fully constructed. The proposal was ratified in early 1881 by the Canadian Parliament in a move that, at last, created the Canadian Pacific Railway.

James J Hill, a Participant

Donald A Smith, a governor of Hudson's Bay company in the Pacific northwest, was named president of the new, privately-held CP system. Smith had asked James J Hill—who had been one of his partners in the Red River Transportation Company in the United States and who would one day build his own railroad empire in the US Pacific northwest—to join him. Hill was named to the executive committee.

Smith and Hill had originally met, so the legend goes, on a snow-covered prairie while driving dog sleds, 150 miles from the nearest house. It was a meeting that would have much effect on the future relations between Canada and the United States. The two were joined by Bank of Montreal President George Stephen. Earlier, Hill had persuaded the two men to invest in his St Paul & Pacific line which had been in decline for years.

While on the board, Hill suggested possible routes the line could take and construction policies as well—but it soon be-

came evident that his motivation was self-interest. When Smith and Stephens decided to keep the main line completely within Canada by building around the north shore of Lake Superior—rather than using Hill's lines through Sault Ste Marie, Ste Paul and Minneapolis to Emerson, Manitoba—Hill resigned from the company.

Although Hill had only spent a short time on the board, his influence was to last for years. Specifically, he had recommended hiring William Cornelius Van Horne to be general manager of the railroad, a man who was to become the hero of the transcontinental project and of the Canadian Pacific Railway.

Van Horne had spent his adult life working on railroads, starting out as a telegraph operator on the Illinois Central at the age of 14. By the age of 27, Van Horne had risen to superintendent of transportation for the Chicago & Alton Railroad. Later, he was named general manager of the bankrupt St Louis, Kansas City & Northern Railroad (later to be called the Wabash), where he demonstrated a flair for financial manage-

Above right: This photo of a Canadian Pacific road crew and their handiwork was taken in 1884, at Morrison's Cut on the north shore of Lake Superior. *Above:* George Stephen, first president of the Canadian Pacific from 1881–1888, was a younger cousin of Canadian Pacific visionary Donald Smith.

ment of railroads by bringing the bankrupt line back to sound financial health. He did the same thing for the Southern Minnesota Railroad as president and general manager.

Van Horne was working for the Southern Minnesota when he was spotted by Hill, who appointed him president of the Chicago, Milwaukee & St Paul Railroad. Van Horne later got a job offer with the Canadian Pacific, became a Canadian citizen, and was eventually knighted by the British Queen for his services to the country.

In Canada, Van Horne went to work immediately to get the project reorganized and under construction again. In 1882, he ordered more than 5000 men in the field with 1700 teams of horses, under the direction of a private firm from St Paul. The firm was commanded to build tracks 900 miles westward from Winnepeg. When work lagged behind schedule, Van Horne put

crews to work at night and increased the number of employees to 10,000—at a time when there were no track-laying machines.

Van Horne was more of an engineer than a businessman. He wanted to construct the shortest route possible from Winnipeg to the Pacific Ocean to complete the work and to get the trains rolling. With Winnipeg as the major supply point, men and materials were supplied from the United States and eastern Canada. Rails came from England by way of New Orleans— up the Mississippi River—while timber and ties were sent from Minnesota and Canada's eastern provinces.

The task of assembling supplies and materials was unusually difficult and costly, as the government found out before handing the project over to private ownership. For instance, locomotives were shipped via the Great Lakes and from there ran under their own steam to the work site.

The first engine used in Manitoba and on the Canadian prairies was the 38-ton *Countess of Dufferin*, a 4–4–0 wood-burner. She had been brought in by way of the Great Lakes to

Port Arthur, then barged to Duluth from where she traveled under her own steam to St Paul and then was transferred to another barge for the trip up the Red River to St Boniface. A second pioneer locomotive, *The JC Haggart*, was hauled up the frozen Red River between St Boniface and Winnepeg in December 1879.

Van Horne set up headquarters in Winnipeg where he managed the operation of the massive project, making sure that supplies and equipment were moved to the railhead as fast as they could be utilized. The work continued at the rate of two to three miles a day as each supply train brought to the front carried enough track and ties to build one mile of track.

Van Horne's genius for organization paid off not only in money but also in time. By the time the building season had ended in the fall of 1880, he had completed 508 miles of track, built 32 stations, strung 807 miles of telegraph wire and was well ahead of schedule.

Van Horne told directors he would build 500 miles of track in his first year on the job, and he delivered as promised. He continued to deliver in succeeding years—his contractors and crews working so swiftly that by the end of 1883 they were pushing their way into the Rockies through Kicking Horse Pass near the US-Canadian border.

Moving westward, Van Horne decided to build well south of Fleming's proposed route to prevent US rail lines from stealing traffic from the Canadians by building close to the border. It was a wise move, in fact, because Hill had wanted the traffic for his own railroad just over the border. Van Horne dropped the idea of using Yellowhead Pass—originally chosen by Fleming—and opted for Kicking Horse Pass. It was a risky decision for Van Horne, as the government contract specified that the grade over the Rockies could be no more than two percent.

The grade on the route ran at 4.5 percent, or a climb of 237 feet to the mile. This violated the contract with the government

but enabled the Canadian Pacific to move ahead. The steep grade remained a part of the system until crews finished construction of the Connaught Tunnel.

Despite generous terms granted by Parliament, the company suffered from cash shortages. Van Horne was able to keep crews working during critical periods when investors ran out of cash—but the workmen did not receive paychecks for several months.

Before the transcontinental line was completed, the directors pledged their private fortunes to keep crews in the field. Then the government came through with a substantial loan. So much money had been invested in the project by Canadian businessmen that, had it gone bankrupt, it might have plunged that nation's economy into a severe recession. But the risks proved lucrative for both the nation and the investors. Dividends were soon paid to the directors, who recouped their investments handsomely.

One of the most difficult track sections for Van Horne was not in the west but in the region around Lake Superior where small lakes and large swamps had to be traversed with rock cut from nearby quarries. The work proved to be as difficult as had been the construction through the Rockies—where a 20-mile grade had to be built above Kicking Horse River.

It was not until 1 November 1885 that regular train service started between Montreal and Winnipeg. The same year, service began between Moose Jaw and Winnipeg, which was a region of granite broken with large tracts of muskeg—swampland that could not sustain the weight of track, much less fully loaded trains.

Van Horne's men surmounted the challenges posed by the muskeg, although in one section the track had to be relaid *seven* times before the ground was stable enough to withstand the weight of a train. It cost twice as much money to construct track around Lake Superior than any other section of line, but Van Horne would not be thwarted. In 1882 he brought his line to Collingwood on Georgia Bay and established steamship service to handle the distribution of supplies and equipment. In winter, portage roads were constructed and supplies brought over by dogsled.

Transcontinental Line Completed

After shutting down for winter, work continued the next year, and by the end of May 1885 the line was essentially complete. The effort had eventually required 12,000 men with 5000 horse teams—and millions of dollars. The first transcontinental train ran in the summer of 1886 after the last spike was driven at Craigellachie, British Columbia on 11 November 1885.

Craigellachie was the name of a famous rock in the Valley of the Sprey River in Scotland. A silver spike was to have been used, but an iron spike was finally driven in a ceremony to celebrate the final linking of the two coasts of Canada.

The ceremony featured Donald A Smith, who gave one of the shortest speeches in railroad history: 'All I can say is that the work has been done well in every way.' The train used at the ceremonies then rolled out—headed for the Pacific—arriving the next day at Burrard Inlet. Regular service began the next year between Montreal and Port Moody.

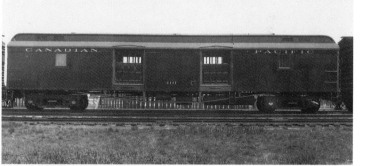

The CP Proves Its Value

Interestingly, the CP proved its value long before it was completed, when it came to the aid of the Canadian government during the second Riel Rebellion in the mid-1880s. The rebellion was led by Louis Riel, the brilliant but vain French-Indian who had gathered a mob around him to capture the Canadian Fur Company's post at Fort Garry.

When rebellion erupted, Van Horne offered to move the government's troops to the scene of the action, enabling the government to save time in putting down the insurrection. But he added one proviso. He wanted complete control of the train movements while moving the troops.

The mission required transporting men and artillery from incomplete sections of the track to sleighs, and back to the terrain again, in 50-degree-below zero weather. Fortunately, Van Horne had learned about troop movement by train during the US Civil War when, as a railroad employee, he had organized and helped moved troops for the Union.

Van Horne's mission was a success—the Canadian troops were unloading at Winnipeg just four days after boarding at Ottawa. When a second detachment of troops was required, the army of men and equipment was also moved along track that was not yet completed—the officers deciding to hold the troops on the train until the work was finished. When the last rail was put in place an army colonel was given the honor of driving the last spike on the railroad's Lake Superior section.

At one point, the train came to a trestle that had not been tested. Only after the train had been emptied of soldiers and equipment did the engine crew take the train across, the troops following behind on the bridge. Eventually they completed this journey and put down the rebellion.

The success of the effort enabled financier Sir John A McDonald to win more financial support for the transcontinental line from the House of Commons, and the Canadian Pacific now gave Canada one of the longest transcontinental lines in North America, running from Montreal in the east to Van-

Note the extreme unevenness of the (swamp area) Port Arthur-Winnipeg RR tracks depicted *above opposite,* **before the Canadian Pacific renovated the line.** *From the top, above:* **Equipment, places and dates on the Canadian Pacific—steam loco, Manitoba, 1940; snow plow, Alberta, 1949; baggage car, BC, 1952; and passenger car, BC, 1968.** *Overleaf:* **A CP freight.**

couver in the west. Comparable trains in the United States had to change in Chicago.

Within three decades of the completion of the Canadian Pacific Railway, the system was one of the biggest and best known in the world and operated a total of more than 22,000 miles of track.

Settlement Began Along the Line

Van Horne refused to give up his US citizenship, but in 1885 he was made president of the Canadian Pacific. While president, Van Horne had designed a house flag that flew from steamship lines on both sides of the continent as well as at company headquarters, reading: 'World's Greatest Travel System.' However, he said he would not remain for long; as soon as the stock of the company rose in par value and as soon as its mileage reached 10,000, he would resign.

He achieved both goals in 1899. As soon as Van Horne resigned as president, Thomas Shaughnessy stepped in as his successor. But Van Horne remained chairman of the board for another 12 years.

Later, he ventured to Cuba, where he constructed that country's first railroad. He agreed to undertake the project even though, in 1900, Cuba was not yet a nation. He completed the work in 1902. He then went to Guatemala where he agreed to direct the completion of a line between Puerto Barrios to Guatemala City. Because of problems associated with insurrections and finances, work was not finished until 1908. Van Horne died in September of 1915.

Despite competition from other railroads, the CP prospered —so much so that the company became the subject of intense scrutiny, and complaints about high rates charged to freight customers by the railroad led the government to consider ending the CP's Canadian rail monopoly. However, the rates remained high.

Dividends were paid from 1885 until the full impact of the Depression hit in 1932. Then no payments were made for 12 years, although the railroad profited from the sale of forest lands that it had been granted by the government during the original construction.

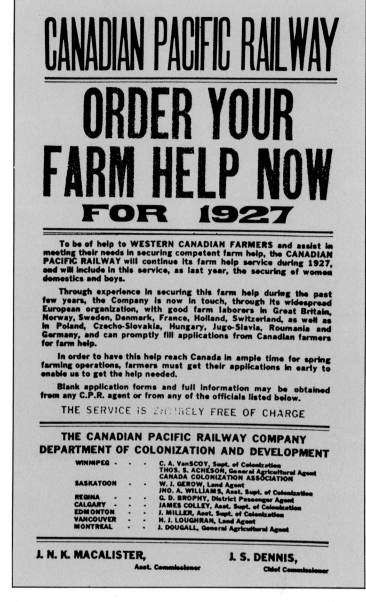

Opposite: A 14 May 1949 Saturday Evening Post ad for the wonders of the Canadian Pacific Railway and its subsidiaries. The lure of the scenic north did in fact draw many a vacationing American across the border. *Above:* Broadsides like this drummed up a lot of rural business.

The early evolution of the Canadian Pacific 'shield' logo. The 'flag' and 'goose' logos represent CP's shipping and airline operations.

After the transcontinental line was opened, Van Horne set about improving connections and branch lines and aquiring smaller lines. The CP set up headquarters in Montreal—the home of its Union Station—and extended service to Quebec, Ontario and Chicago. The CP also extended lines to the Maritime provinces, adding a connection to St John.

In the west, the CP constructed connections with the United States south of Vancouver. It also bought control of two US lines that ran from Sault Ste Marie, Michigan, permitting an easy connection over the St Mary's River and ship locks. The St Paul & Sault Ste Marie Railway gave connections to St Paul, Minnesota and thence northwest to Canada. This blocked the competing Grand Trunk Railway from moving into its territory.

Meanwhile, in the west, problems erupted between the railroad and its neighbors. The province of Manitoba, which did not favor dominance by the Canadian Pacific, granted charters to several provincial railways. This was done despite the fact that the CP had been given the right to operate without competition for more than 20 years. As a consequence, a battle erupted at Fort Whyte between the Canadian Pacific and the Red River Valley Railway—one of the lines authorized by the provincial government—when the provincial line needed to cross the CP line at grade.

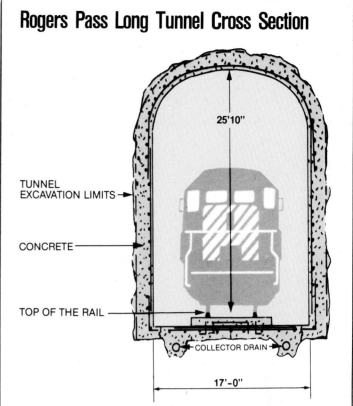

Rogers Pass Long Tunnel Cross Section

TUNNEL EXCAVATION LIMITS →

25'10"

CONCRETE →

TOP OF THE RAIL →

← COLLECTOR DRAIN →

17'-0"

Below left: A CP Rail container freight at Albert Canyon, BC. The CP Rail freight *at left* skirts the Sawback Range (in background) near Banff, Alberta. *Above:* CP Rail construction workers prepare for another round of blasting as they begin the Rogers Pass Tunnel on Mount MacDonald.

The first crossing was installed by the Red River Valley, but was immediately taken out by CP crews and taken to a CP yard. Crewmen also deliberately derailed a provincial locomotive (there were no injuries). The standoff lasted for more than two weeks before CP crews relented, allowing the provincial railroad to cross the CP's tracks.

By 1900 the CP was quickly becoming a major carrier of wheat, a world commodity and shipping facilities were developed on the Great Lakes. Other facilities were constructed at Montreal and other ocean ports.

The CP had a trans-Pacific steamship service soon after completion of the transcontinental work. In 1889 the British government granted CP the right to carry mail between Vancouver and Hong Kong. In 1891 the CP used three ocean liners—*The Empress of India, The Empress of China* and *The Empress of Japan*—to make voyages across the Pacific Ocean. Later the CP entered steamship service in the Atlantic.

The Canadian Pacific continued to expand its empire. It bought other rail lines and built luxury hotels. In 1902 it introduced a fast continental passenger train, *The Imperial Limited,* to supplement the original service provided by *The Pacific Express* and *The Atlantic Express.* In 1919, the first all-Pullman diner train made the trip between Montreal, Toronto and Vancouver on CP tracks.

In 1983 CP Rail began work on its $600 million Rogers Pass Project, the largest to be undertaken since the completion of the transcontinental tracks in the 1880s. When completed in the early 1990s, the tunnel will be the largest in North America. The project includes double tracking and the construction of a nine-mile tunnel through the Selkirk Mountains in British Columbia. The project will reduce the approach grade for westbound trains from the current 2.2 percent grade on the steepest parts of the line.

The Rogers Pass Project is the latest in a series of improvements. After 1900 the CP made major improvements to its main line through the Rocky Mountains, especially the steep descent known as the 'Big Hill' through Kicking Horse Pass.

Eastbound trains were forced to climb it by dividing up their cars and using smaller locomotives to pull them up the hill in sections.

Workmen constructed two spiral tunnels that were completed in 1909 and are world famous. The first was constructed under the Cathedral Mountains. More than 3000 feet long, it curves more than 234 degrees in its descent of 48 feet between entrance and exit. The second tunnel drops 45 feet and makes a 232 degree turn through the mountains from entrance to exit. It is almost 3000 feet long. Construction of the tunnels enabled the railway to reduce the grade up Kicking Horse pass to 2.2 percent.

In 1916 the Connaught Tunnel, five miles long, was completed. This major tunnel enabled trains to avoid the many curves on the west side of the Beaver River through Rogers Pass. The original line had been plagued by landslides and caused many accidents. Later the pass served as the route of the Trans Canadian Highway.

The Canadian Pacific set the standards for intermountain locomotives. The company introduced locomotives of its own design that were perfect for working the grades over the Rocky Mountains between Calgary and Vancouver. These were a class of 2–10–4 that could be favorably compared to any of the locomotives in use in the United States.

The Montreal Locomotives Works constructed 36 of these machines, originally built to burn coal but later converted to burn oil. CPR also used a series of 2–6–0s, 4–6–0s and 4–6–2s. The 1200 class of 4–6–2s were especially popular. They were used by the system until the advent of diesels in the 1940s. The CP also set the standard for rolling stock and locomotives and was especially known for its observation cars, first introduced in 1919 after World War I.

The Depression was an especially difficult time for the CP, because dividends had to be cut in the face of dwindling traffic. When government officials were obliged to examine the cost of maintaining competitive railroads in that time of great economic distress, some thought was given to eliminating

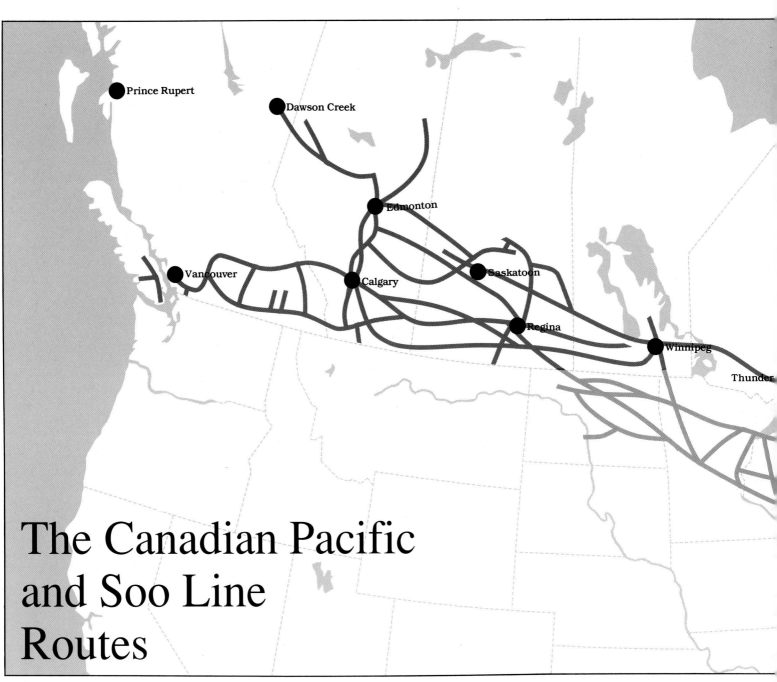

Prince Rupert

Dawson Creek

Edmonton

Vancouver

Calgary

Saskatoon

Regina

Winnipeg

Thunder

The Canadian Pacific and Soo Line Routes

competitive routes to save money, especially in the eastern sections of the country—for example, running duplicate passenger service between Toronto and Montreal.

In the 1930s, following an investigation by a Royal Commission, the Canadian National Railway (CN) and the Canadian Pacific Railway (CP) agreed to pool passenger train service between Montreal and Toronto and between Ottowa and Toronto.

World War II

Like the other railroads of North America, the CP and the CN were pushed to the limit to meet the demands of World War II. In 1944 the two railroads set a record for carrying passengers—60 million. Post-war adjustments were especially difficult for the CP when the demand to carry freight and passengers quickly dropped off and buses, trucks and commercial air traffic began to siphon off rail traffic. The management of the CP organized an airline subsidiary in 1942, taking over some bush airlines in northern Canada, then expanding service outside Canada a few years later.

The decline in rail traffic was exacerbated following a lengthy strike in 1950. Although it lasted only nine days, it had a profound effect. Shippers turned to trucks to haul perishable goods during this period. They found that the service was as good if not better than the train service—and they never went back.

Both the CP and the CN fought back in the 1950s, introducing faster transcontinental service on passenger trains. The CP introduced a train known as *The Canadian*, which featured all-diesel locomotives, streamlined stainless steel coaches and dome cars in every train. The CN then followed with *The Super-Continental*. Cross-country train times were reduced by as much as 16 hours because the new diesel locomotives did not stop as often as the steam locomotives for refueling and maintenance.

As traffic continued to decline through the 1950s and 1960s, Canadian Pacific officials decided that the rail traffic no longer justified the cost of running operations such as its famed *Canadian* service and asked for permission to drop it.

The last steam locomotive run took place in May 1960, although CP kept a few steam locomotives in working order for another decade, to be used for special occasions.

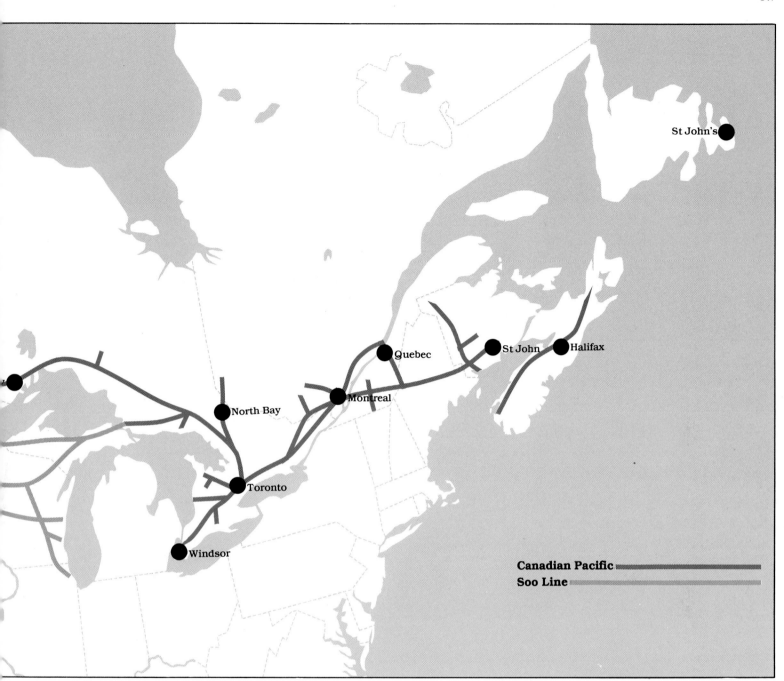

St John's

Quebec

Montreal

North Bay

St John   Halifax

Toronto

Windsor

Canadian Pacific ▬▬▬▬▬▬▬▬
Soo Line ▬▬▬▬▬▬▬▬

VIA

Today, passenger trains in Canada are operated much like passenger trains in the United States—under the control of a government corporation. In the United States, the corporation is known as Amtrak. In Canada, the crown corporation is known as VIA Rail Canada, Inc.

VIA became independent of both the Canadian Pacific and the Canadian National on 1 April 1978, and since that time it has taken the responsibility for managing all of Canada's rail passenger service—except for subway systems and commuter lines. Montreal is the national headquarters for VIA.

The Canadian Pacific sold VIA more than 300 passenger rail cars to get the government service started. Although VIA owns no track, it operates over the tracks of other railroads and employs more than 4000 workers. Meanwhile, locomotive engineers, brakemen and conductors remain on the payroll of either the CP or the CN. VIA operates over more than 14,000 miles of track with regular passenger service.

At right: VIA Rail is the Canadian equivalent of the US Amtrak—a government run railroad that handles a nation's entire passenger service.

CANADIAN NATIONAL

A Crown Corporation

Canada is unique in having two great railway systems, one privately held and the other government held. The privately held railroad, CP Rail, is one of Canada's largest and most successful corporations. The Dominion government created the Canadian National Railway Company as a Crown Corporation in 1919 to ensure that Canada would always have the transportation necessary for their vast country.

At that time—just after the end of World War I—several of Canada's largest railroads were financially weak and unable to continue operating independently. The government decided to incorporate them into a single railroad with stronger financial resources and access to government capital. Since then, the system has become one of Canada's most successful corporations and has branched out into other transportation fields.

In fact, the Canadian National, most of whose $5 billion in assets is deployed in transportation, is one of Canada's largest corporations. CN is organized into a number of divisions, including CN Communications, CN Trucking, CN Express, CN Hotels and Tower, CN Marine and TerraTransport. The railway arm of Canadian National is called CD Rail. Altogether, CN is one of Canada's largest employers.

CN Rail operates a fleet of 2200 diesel locomotives, 92,000 cars of all types and over 25,000 miles of track, making it one of the largest single railroads in the world.

Above left: Canadian National freight locomotives in the yard at Taschereau Yard in Montreal. *At right:* CN lift trucks move containers from trucks to trains—for further transfer to container ships—in St John's, Newfoundland. Containerization has revolutionized the entire freight transport industry.

The Beginnings

While the CN is government held, many railroads comprising CN Rail were once private systems. The history of the combined railroad is the story of the growth of the Canadian transportation system.

One hundred and fifty years ago, Canada was a much different country. It was a virgin landscape of impassable mountains, impenetrable swamps and bogs, and vast forests full of huge trees. Communities were isolated for many months of the year, separated by long, harsh winters of bitter cold and blizzards. The narrow roads linking settlements were wholly in-

Below: The Canadian National ran this oil-electric engine—which is actually a double unit, joined tail to tail—in 1928. Compare this engine to the modern CN diesel freight engine *above,* which was photographed near Lytton, British Columbia. This is a case of one new idea developing into another.

adequate—when it rained the road mud churned too deeply and slippery to be traversed, and travelers were forced to wait for days before roads dried sufficiently.

In the first half of the 19th century, Halifax, Quebec City and Montreal were Canada's most important cities, but all three depended upon waterways for supplies and goods. Every winter the ice blocked the ships and boats from navigating on rivers and lakes, while business slowed to a standstill and communities had little choice but to wait until the ice cleared for transportation services to recover.

Summers were better, but settlers had to endure difficulties and delays caused by rapids and waterfalls. In some locations, canals were constructed to bypass problem areas, but for the most part, settlers had to depend on the rivers and lakes for transportation.

Businessmen in Upper and Lower Canada and the Maritime provinces desperately needed more reliable transportation to ship their supplies and to move people. Ships and boats from Europe and the United States sailed as far up the St Lawrence

River as Montreal, a distance of 800 kilometers. They brought linens, china, clothing, machinery and other household goods needed by the Canadian settlers. When the roads were dry, stagecoaches and carts carried supplies and passengers.

On the Great Lakes, settlers used boats to connect cities and towns, while in the far west, large canoes capable of holding up to 12 men were used. With such a diversity of undependable transportation to rely upon, it is no wonder that Canadians followed the development of the steam-powered railroad in the United States and England with great interest.

In 1832, a group of businessmen known as the 'The Company of Proprietors' built Canada's first railroad—the Champlain & St Lawrence—which carried its first traffic in 1836. When the first trains started running, there was great celebration, with hundreds of people eager to take rides. The Champlain & St Lawrence operated from the town of Saint-Jean on the Richelieu River, then north to the St Lawrence near Montreal, a distance of just 23 kilometers. Constructed to replace the main road and river links between Montreal and New York City, the Champlain & St Lawrence circumvented the rapids on the Richelieu River which had prevented boats from navigating up Lake Champlain to Montreal.

The Champlain & St Lawrence Railroad's first locomotive was imported from England, just as railroad engines in the United States had been. Called *The Dorchester*, it was a wood-burning steam engine with a tall smokestack. But it proved unreliable, managing on its first test run to pull only two of the six passenger coaches. The other cars had to be hauled by horses.

Despite problems with the locomotive, the Champlain & St Lawrence Railroad was successful. The locomotive, about the size of a small automobile today, covered the distance between Saint Jean and the St Lawrence in about 30 minutes. The stage coach, in the best of times, had required about three hours. The railroad was profitable because of the steady flow of passengers who wanted to ride the train and because merchants wanted to move goods by rail.

Motivated by the success of the Champlain and St Lawrence, the government over the next 15 years granted permission to more than 40 companies to construct railroads. Yet, by 1850, only six were operating or laying track and the government realized that railroads were not yet profitable in Canada.

Lack of capital proved a major stumbling block to most of small railroads. Canadian business and industry did not have enough resources to raise the capital necessary to build a railroad system, so the money had to be borrowed from England or the United States.

It cost money to survey the routes, clear and level the land, and then build the tracks. That was not all. Before

entrepreneurs could operate trains and recoup their investments, they had to purchase and import locomotives, freight cars and passenger cars from the United States or England. But not enough people were living and working in Canada yet to justify the cost and expense.

Of the six railroads that managed to put down track, three were short lines built to avoid obstructions along river transportation routes. These were the Champlain & St Lawrence, the Erie & Ontario and the Montreal & Lachine railroads, which avoided the rapids on the St Lawrence River.

When this last mentioned railroad started operating, the engineer, a Scotsman, was so proud of the new Scottish-built locomotives that he took dignitaries and guests along the track at speeds approaching 100 kilometers per hour, managing to terrify everyone. The force of the wind at those speeds crushed the hats of the men and the hoop skirts of the women.

The St Lawrence & Atlantic Railroad was the biggest project started before 1850. Two companies combined to build the railroad—one Canadian and one American. The two wanted to construct a 480-kilometer line connecting Lonueuil—across the river from Montreal—with Portland, Maine where the nearest ice-free port was located. However, the Canadians ran out of money and the work had to be halted.

The government soon realized that if Canada was to build a viable railroad network, it would have to help finance the construction and purchase of equipment. In 1849 the governments of Upper and Lower Canada promised assistance, offering to pay for half the cost of railroads that were more than 120 kilometers long.

When adopted, this legislation enabled private investors to complete the St Lawrence & Atlantic Railroad, while other investors started up other railroads. The result was that in the following 65 years, more than 56,000 kilometers of track were constructed between the Atlantic and Pacific oceans in a network which united Canada in just such a manner as track had connected the eastern and western United States.

In the 1850s, Upper and Lower Canada experienced an explosion of railroad construction. Small lines as well as long lines were constructed to link major cities within the eastern provinces. The Great Western Railway (GW) started building two lines in Upper Canada, with one line running from Hamilton to Niagara Falls and the other from Hamilton to London.

The original company had struggled since 1834. Yet, the Great Western Railway started laying track only after the government stepped in with financial aid. Within a few years, the railroad operated 580 kilometers of track from Toronto south to Windsor, Sarnia and Niagara Falls. The lines were important to Upper Canada because they provided critical trade links between the United States and the province.

Interestingly, two early but major train accidents occurred on lines operated by the Great Western. In 1854, two trains collided near Chatham, killing 47 crewmen and passengers. Three years later, 60 people died when a bridge collapsed over the Desjardins Canal near Hamilton. Despite the widespread loss of life, the accidents did not discourage progress.

The Great Western constructed Canada's first railroad suspension bridge, a span stretching across the Niagara River. With a main span of 250 meters, the bridge was hailed as an engineering marvel.

Canada's most important railway was established in the 1850s. Called the Grand Trunk Railway Company of Canada, the road was to become one of the nation's most successful. The name 'Grand Trunk' was derived from the original plan by company officials to operate one mainline railroad, to be connected to smaller lines much like the branches of a tree joined to a trunk.

Construction proved to be expensive, but because of capital provided by English businessmen the line was completed and survived. Another rail line was constructed from a railhead east of Quebec City to Sarnia, connecting Montreal and Toronto. The job included construction of the world famous Victoria Bridge across the St Lawrence, which was completed in 1856 and eventually reached Portland, Maine. So important was the opening of the Grand Trunk from Montreal to Toronto that 4000 people attended a banquet to celebrate the event.

Maritime Provinces

The Maritime provinces found railroad start-ups more difficult to finance and build. Plans had been drawn as early as 1827 to construct tracks between St Andrews on the Bay of Fundy and Quebec City. Because there was no clear border between the United States and Canada, political problems erupted when the US government protested that the line would trespass on American territory. So to avoid controversy, the Canadians abandoned it.

Attempts were made in the early 1850s to get the project going again—this time between Portland (Maine) and Halifax. However, only a few kilometers had been constructed when the Great Western ran out of cash. Another line—the Nova Scotia Railway—was finally constructed between Halifax, Truro and Windsor in 1854 using unusual rails for its system—they were shaped the same on both top and bottom so that when one side became worn the other could be used.

In the 1860s the Maritime provinces constructed more than 3000 kilometers of track, enabling passengers to travel by train all the way from Riviere du Loup to Sarnia in one trip. But it was not a pleasant experience as the rails were just 5.5 meters long with wide gaps between them. This jolted passengers aboard the cars. First class travelers had cushioned seats, which helped, but second class passengers had to endure hard wood bench seats.

Dining cars did not exist, so trains had to stop at stations for meals and again at night to allow travelers to find hotels. The first sleeping car in the world was designed and constructed in Hamilton by the Great Western Railway. This original version was uncomfortable compared to later models; it was simply a long wooden box car with long benches. Travelers were given rugs and pillows and directed to the nearest bench.

Train crews suffered as many hardships as the passengers did in the early days of Canadian railroading. For instance,

Opposite: An early-to mid-20th century CN 2–8–2 Mikado type locomotive, originally built for export to Japan. *Below:* This NP oil-electric locomotive headed Train Number 25 on the Moncton-Campbelltown, New Brunswick run in 1937. *Above:* A 1930 ad for the CN.

Above: The Canadian Northern was, as of this 1930s-era photograph, the largest constituent part of the CN. Shown here is a freight yard in Saskatoon, Saskatchewan. *Above right:* A CN passenger diesel, circa 1954. *Below right:* The CN's triple-stacking automobile transport system.

firemen were required to throw heavy logs into the firebox, and whenever they had a free moment they had to climb outside on the engine to grease the bearings. They were also required to load the wood boxes at each stop as well as free the ashes from the firebox of the locomotive. When trains ran late, even the passengers were asked to step out and load wood to speed the trip.

In smaller towns and villages, the arrival of the train was the big event of the day. When the train reached the station, people crowded around it to stare at the wealthy travelers and perhaps chat with the passengers who got out to stroll. Young engineers were greeted by pretty girls at each stop, and the townspeople enjoyed catching up on the latest news and gossip reported by the crewmen.

Like pioneer American railroads, early Canadian lines helped to improve the living conditions of citizens living far away from the big cities. Before the arrival of the train, earning money was difficult; but once a line was opened, the farmers could earn money by shipping their produce to market by train. In that way, eggs, butter, milk, fruit, chicken and other farm products were shipped to the cities in exchange for cash. Local craftsmen sold their work to travelers, and farmers were often paid to provide wood for the locomotives. In short, a new rail line meant prosperity and growth for everyone.

The railroads also built telegraph lines to send messages from one station to another. They were often used to warn workers of problems on the line and to forecast train arrivals. The trains themselves brought newspapers, magazines and letters from the outside world and helped to connect villages and towns with one another.

When the time came to build a railroad connecting the eastern provinces with western Canada, the efforts of railroad entrepreneurs became one of the most important chapters in the history of Canada. Some historians believe, if fact, that had the line not been constructed, the western province of British Columbia would have joined the United States. The project almost went broke, and several times the necessary funds were raised just in time to keep it going. Many men died in the effort. However, in 1885, the last spike was driven into the ground to create the 4666-kilometer Canadian Pacific line.

By the turn of the century, Canadians had accomplished a great deal with their railroad network. In just 50 years, the railroad system had grown from only 130 kilometers of track to more than 27,350. Iron rails had been replaced with steel, and wooden bridges were replaced with iron. Then coal replaced wood in steam locomotives, allowing them to run farther without stopping to refuel.

In 1901 the Canadian government recognized that the nation needed more settlers to bolster the economy, especially in the western prairies and mountains. The government therefore started a campaign to advertise for immigrants from Europe, and huge posters were slapped up all over the towns of England and the major European cities.

Thousands of people began pouring into Canada, most heading for the wide open lands of the west. Soon, new towns and settlements sprang up along the rail lines, along with

farms, mining and lumber companies. The discovery of a new strain of wheat which ripens two weeks earlier than other varieties encouraged farmers to relocate farther north. The discovery doubled the amount of land that could be farmed in the prairies and created demands for new railroads.

In the early 1900s, two Ontario men, William MacKenzie and Donald Mann, built the Canadian Northern Railroad from Portage la Prairie in Manitoba north to Dauphin. When completed, they bought another line running west from Thunder Bay to Winnepeg. By 1905, their rails had crossed the Canadian prairie to Edmonton.

They were underfinanced, and construction was not always up to standard. In ensuing years, crews would have to go back and reconstruct much of the track; but completion of the project helped unite eastern and western Canada. By 1915, MacKenzie and Mann had extended their Canadian Northern Railway all the way to Vancouver. It was one of the stunning achievements of Canadian railroad construction.

MacKenzie and Mann were not the only entrepreneurs at work in this era. In 1905, work started on the Grand Trunk Pacific, the third railroad to connect the east with the Pacific coast of Canada. The Grand Trunk Pacific constructed its mainline to Edmonton from Winnipeg, then utilized Yellowhead Pass in British Columbia to reach the Pacific coast. Because Canada had two existing railroads closely paralleling each other, the Grand Trunk Pacific decided to go directly west (rather than west, then south to Vancouver), reaching the Pacific Ocean some 885 kilometers north of Vancouver. They named the terminus there Prince Rupert.

To encourage settlements, the Grand Trunk Pacific decided to build stations every 24 kilometers along the line. The railroad believed that farmers should not have to travel more than 12 kilometers to reach one of its depots. Stations were given names in alphabetical order from east to west. At many locations, however, the towns and cities did not materialize as planned, and today the waysigns are merely names with small settlements. Most western Canadian cities take their names from the men who helped to construct the railroad.

While gangs worked on the Grand Trunk Pacific, the Canadian government had other men laying a mainline from Moncton in New Brunswick to Winnepeg as part of the National Transcontinental Railway. The route, built far to the north of Montreal and Toronto, was costly because of the problems of building around lakes and swamps. Although there were no settlements or cities along this route, it was the shortest coast-to-coast route in Canada.

Consolidation

The year 1915 was an historic one for Canada's railways. The National Transcontinental, the Canadian Northern and the Grand Trunk Pacific inaugurated cross-country routes in the same year, giving Canada more than 56,000 kilometers of lines; but it was a costly achievement. The nation now had

many lines, but there was not enough business to keep them profitable.

With the war in Europe under way, something had to be done to keep Canada's nationwide network of railways operating; and with the war effort, the routes were needed more than ever. But the railroads—with the exception of the Canadian Pacific—were so far in debt that they faced the possibility of shutting down.

To save its investment, the government decided to step in and take over the operation of many rail lines that were in trouble. In 1919, an act was passed creating a new company owned by the people of Canada and called the Canadian National Railway Company. The largest lines of the new system were the Intercolonial, the Grand Trunk, the Grand Trunk Pacific, the National Transcontinental and the Canadian Northern.

The Grand Trunk

One of three Canadian-owned railroads operating in the United States—the Grand Trunk Western, the Central Vermont and the Duluth, Winnipeg & Pacific railways—the Grand Trunk was the largest and most important, serving many of America's largest industrial cities such as Chicago, Detroit, Toledo and Milwaukee.

The Grand Trunk Western (GTW) began back in the 1850s when Grand Trunk of Canada opted to move into the north central region of the United States. The first section connected Port Huron and Detroit, enabling goods and passengers to travel between the two cities.

By the 1870s, GTW directors decided to build their own connection between Chicago and Canada rather than continue to pay high charges to American railroad baron William Vanderbilt for the right to use his tracks and equipment. In 1879, therefore, the Grand Trunk purchased the Chicago and Port Huron Railroad (C&PH), thereby gaining a direct connection to the Windy City.

The purchase effectively foiled Vanderbilt's scheme of driving out competition in the midwest. The new company was

renamed the Chicago and Grand Trunk Railway, but the name was again changed to the Grand Trunk Western. (It became part of Canadian National in 1923.) Grand Trunk lines meet those of the Canadian National in southwestern Ontario at Windsor and Sarnia. The interchange of the Canadian National and Grand Trunk Western equipment occurs at Sarnia and Port Huron, and the GTW interchange with CP&H equipment occurs south of the Detroit River between Windsor and Detroit. Nine other short lines, all in Michigan, were added in 1928.

Although familiar with all kinds of freight loadings, the Grand Trunk carries, for the most part, automobiles and automotive parts for manufacturers in the midwestern US region. For example, thousands of tons of steel, plastic and other parts are carried to plants in Michigan. On the return trip, automobiles and trucks are shipped by rail to dealers all over North America.

The Central Vermont Railway

The Central Vermont Railway connects Quebec with New London, Connecticut, crossing five US states—Connecticut, New York, Massachusetts, New Hampshire and Vermont—in the process. The Central Vermont had its beginnings in 1848, when the Champlain and St Lawrence began carrying traffic. Several Vermont businessmen, who needed to ship goods to markets in Montreal and New York, created the railroad.

The Grand Trunk bought into the Central Vermont in the late 1890s, and when Canadian National took over the Grand Trunk in 1923 it inherited the Central Vermont. It continued to operate as a separate unit until 1927 when new capital was needed to repair damage done by severe winter storms (more than 25 percent of the track had been destroyed by heavy rains and flooding). Canadian National sent 2500 men into action to repair tracks and equipment; three months later the line reopened and shortly thereafter the Canadian National purchased the line.

Today, the Central Vermont is a critical link between Montreal and New York City. It is also eastern Canada's connection with major New England cities.

The Duluth, Winnipeg & Pacific Railway

Despite its name, the Duluth, Winnipeg & Pacific (DW&P) Railway has no connections to the Pacific coast. It starts in Duluth, Minnesota and runs to the Canadian border. The original line was just 150 kilometers long, constructed by American businessmen who wanted a fast, reliable way to ship lumber from forests around the Great Lakes to midwestern cities.

Railroads similar to the DW&P were constructed to connect forests and mining centers to large cities. Usually when trees and ore were exhausted, the rail links were shut down. But the DW&P survived.

When William MacKenzie and Donald Mann of the Canadian Northern Railway completed their line from Thunder Bay to Winnipeg, they bought the DW&P because it ran close to the Canadian-US border. They then extended it south from Virginia, Minnesota—near the Canadian border—to Duluth and north from Virginia to Fort Frances, Ontario where it joined with the Canadian Northern. Completed in 1912, the DW&P carries newsprint, potash and many other goods to the United States.

Modern Origins of the CN

After 1923, Canadian National became one of the largest railroads in the world, featuring more than 35,000 kilometers of track and operating more than 13,000 cars and equipment and 2000 locomotives. But it was not without its major problems—many routes had been built close together, so duplicate rail had to be eliminated while time tables, work rules and salaries had to be adjusted to make them uniform nationally, and employees who had competed against each other were forced to work in unison for the good of the newly-unified system.

American citizen Henry Thornton, who had worked for the British during the war, was hired to merge the disparate railroads into a cohesive network. A very progressive and far-sighted man, Thornton introduced many reforms and changes. For instance, the Canadian National was the first railroad in North America to build a diesel electric locomotive designed to run long distances. To attract new immigrants to regions served by the Canadian National, Thornton created a special service to help them find jobs and to adjust to their new life.

Thornton created the first radio network in Canada to entertain passengers during cross-country trips. He ordered special radio cars constructed in which passengers could wear headsets to listen to programs selected by a radio operator. Thornton's system was later taken over by the Canadian Broadcasting Company.

One of CN's more unusual assignments occured in the 1920s when it deployed special trains to carry raw silk from Vancouver—where it was off-loaded from Japan—to New York City, where it was processed into expensive clothing. Raw silk rots quickly if not processed within a few days, so the fastest ships were pressed into service to sail from Japan to Vancouver. From there, Canadian National trains sped across Canada with special authority. Slower trains were ordered onto sidings as the silk trains moved eastward, stopping only 10 minutes at a time for fuel and water; the trip took less than 80 hours coast to coast.

The 1920s were also an era of prosperity for the CN, due to the millions of tons of grain it moved from the prairies to Canada's large seaports. In 1929, new rail service was provided to the port of Churchill on the Hudson Bay.

The construction of the Hudson Bay line from The Pas, Manitoba to Churchill had begun in 1909. At the time, it presented major engineering challenges because of the mushy, treacherous terrain involved. The extremely unstable ground surface required the frequent rebuilding of many sections of track. In fact, a supply train once slid off the track and was literally sucked into the muck. Its crew members saved themselves, fortunately, but their train, loaded with supplies and materials, simply disappeared! Other crewmen faced derailments, collapsed bridges, epidemics, brushfires and floods, not to mention rampaging moose and ravaging wolves where were attracted to the work camps by the smell of freshly cooked food.

Work on this line was finally completed in 1929, 20 years after construction first got underway. Ironically, though it took less time for ships to reach Europe from Churchill, Thunder Bay remained the largest center for handling grain shipments after the completion of the project.

CN Expands in the 1920s

The CN did more than handle grain and silk. Each fall during the harvest season, the CN brought in hundreds of young men from eastern Canada to the western farms to help harvest the wheat. At each stop on the prairie, farmers would come to the train, pick out the strongest, hardiest-looking workers, and offer them jobs. The CN often allowed hobos and other jobless men to travel for free to the prairie for temporary work with the harvest.

The Depression was a crucial period for the CN. The number of passengers dwindled because Canadians did not have the money to travel, while the number of hobos and other itinerants increased as men moved from city to city looking for jobs. When they couldn't find any, they slept in box cars. Meanwhile, grain traffic, one of the major revenue sources for the CN, fell off dramatically.

The end of the Depression was signaled by the beginning of World War II. From 1939 to 1945, Canadian National carried

Left, opposite: CN hopper cars are unloaded of wood chips by an overhead pneumatic system in Quebec. Note the French Canadian CN logo on the car at left. Bright yellow sulfur dominates this view *(right, opposite)* of two CN freights in British Columbia. *Below:* The CN's MacMillan freight yard in Toronto.

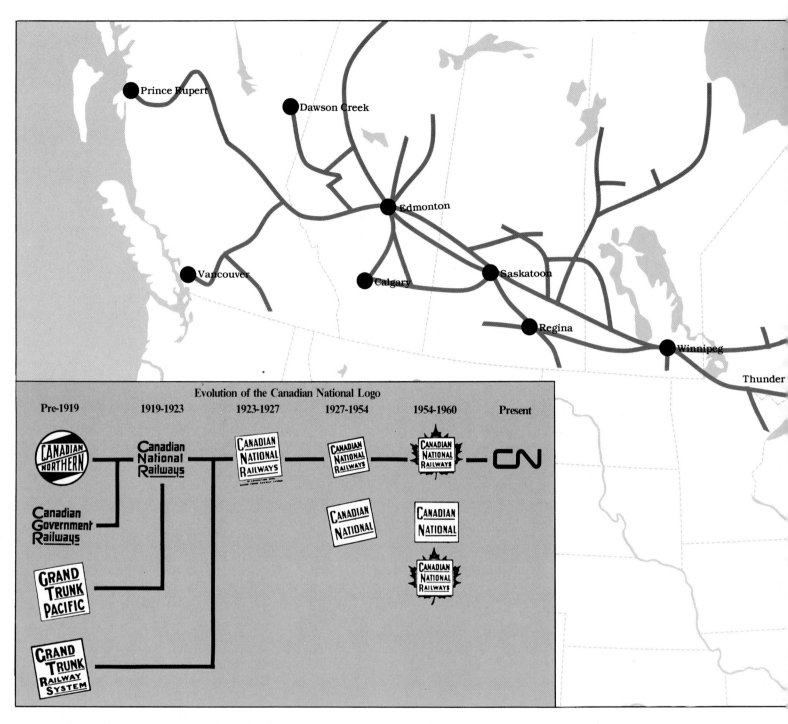

Prince Rupert

Dawson Creek

Edmonton

Vancouver

Calgary

Saskatoon

Regina

Winnipeg

Thunder

Evolution of the Canadian National Logo

| Pre-1919 | 1919-1923 | 1923-1927 | 1927-1954 | 1954-1960 | Present |

Owned by the Canadian National Corporation, the Grand Trunk operates from Port Huron to Chicago, Detroit, Toledo, Cincinnati, Muskegon, Lansing and other points in the northern US, forming the lowest branch system on the CN route map *above*. *Below opposite:* A GT loco passes through the 'carwash.'

wartime goods and soldiers. Traffic actually doubled, and demand was so great that the old cars and equipment had to be taken from retirement and pressed into service. Women were employed to replace the 20,000 male workers who were called into uniform to fight the war.

During the six years of conflict, few locomotives and no new cars were constructed. Consequently, when the war ended the CN system began to fall apart. Many of its locomotives and cars were run down and worn out, and there was little money for replacement. The CN was put in the position of spending a great deal of money to make itself even barely competitive in the postwar era. Meanwhile, the trucking industry had begun.

It soon became a major means of transportation, taking business away from the CN. In addition, increasing numbers of Canadians were using automobiles and airplanes rather than trains.

To compete effectively, Canadian National ordered specialized cars and rolling stock. Shippers liked these new cars because they were easier to load and unload and could carry more freight. New diesel locomotives were ordered and brought into service because they were cheaper to operate and maintain than steam engines. Even radar and computers were added in rail yards to speed the sorting and maintenance of cars; the CN also installed thousands of miles of electronically controlled switches so that trains could operate faster and closer together.

In 1949, when Newfoundland joined the Confederation, the CN took over its rail lines, most of which were narrow gauge, and remain so. CN also began operating ferries between Nova Scotia and the new island province. It was during this period that the CN started to construct new lines in the west to link with the mining region along the Arctic Circle.

The most successful new line, the Great Slave Lake Railway, stretches from northern Alberta into the Northwest Ter-

The Canadian National and Grand Trunk Western Routes

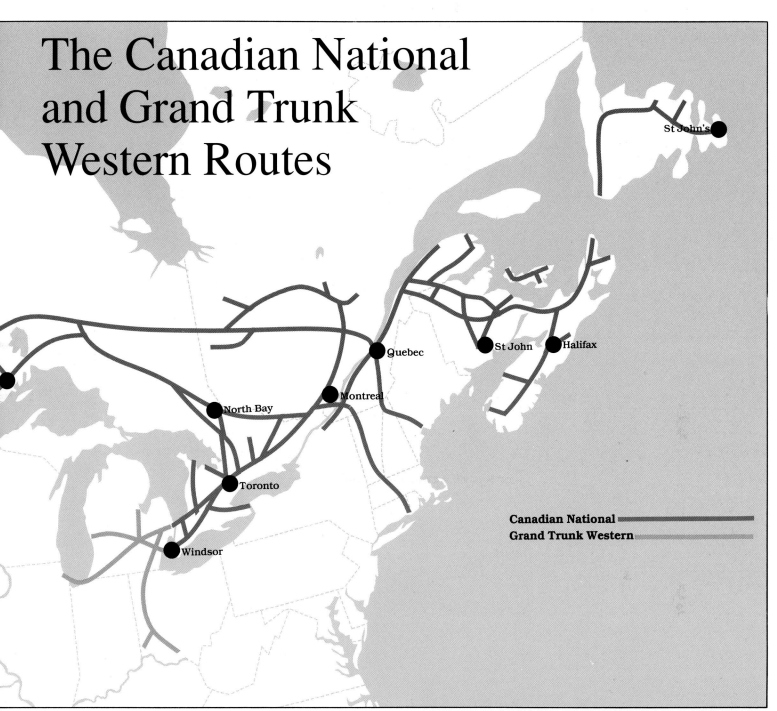

Canadian National ▬▬▬▬▬
Grand Trunk Western ▬▬▬▬▬

ritories. The 432 miles of this railway were constructed from 1962 to 1964 to tap the resources the of the vast Northwest Territories such as the zinc and lead deposits around Pine Point and to ship ore to smelters in British Columbia.

The Great Slave was constructed mostly in winter, sometimes with temperatures as low as 47 degrees below zero F. The main piece of track-laying equipment was an automated machine that not only laid and secured rails but pulled a seven-car worktrain—including flatcars loaded with rail, ties and fastenings. With a 50-man crew, it laid track at the rate of one mile a day, or 12 feet per minute.

The CN rebuilt itself from the ground up, moving swiftly to maintain its importance to Canadians. Railroad land was leased for the building of new industrial parks and shopping centers; old hotels owned by the CN system were renovated or rebuilt and new hotels were constructed.

Today the CN operates a fleet of ferries and coastal vessels and provides a wide range of national and international consulting services. Indeed, Canadian National has grown as Canada has grown.

CSX CORPORATION

The CSX Corporation

The CSX Corporation is an unusual name for a railroad, but it represents a major trend in American railroading—the wave of consolidation and mergers which occurred in the 1980s. CSX is the name given to the merger in 1980 of the Chessie System, Inc and Seaboard Coast Line Industries, Inc. In turn, these two holding companies represent the merger of many different rail lines and systems, several originating in the earliest days of railroading.

The Chessie controls six railroad systems—the Chesapeake & Ohio, the Baltimore & Ohio, the Western Maryland, the B&O Chicago Terminal, the Staten Island & Chicago South Shore and the South Bend—reaching from the Atlantic Ocean to St Louis on the Mississippi River and from West Virginia to Canada. The Chessie operates more than 50,000 freight cars over more than 11,200 miles of track.

Seaboard Coast Line Industries (SCLI) is the holding company for the Family Lines System of 10 railroads located in the southeast, including the Seaboard Coast Line, the Louisville & Nashville (L&N), the Clinchfield, the Georgia, the Western Railway of Alabama, the Atlanta & West Point, the Durham & Southern and the Newberry & Laurens.

The CSX also controls the Richmond, Fredericksburg & Potomac Railway which connects the northern US to southern rail systems. The Family Lines System operates trains on over 15,000 miles of track.

Most of CSX's 17 railroads operate independently, but offer coordinated transportation services to freight customers. The CSX Corp operates more than 27,000 miles of track throughout 22 states including the District of Columbia and the Canadian province of Ontario.

Because of its strategic location in the southeast, the CSX is America's largest hauler of coal. It contributes 40 percent of the Chessie's business and 20 percent of the Seaboard's business and has more than $7 billion in assets.

One reason for the merger creating CSX was the need to save costs. It was estimated that the combined operation would save nearly 15 million gallons annually in fuel by allowing more efficient operations over the wide area covered by the CSX.

Chesapeake & Ohio

Some executives claim that George Washington, the first president of the United States and America's great Revolutionary War hero, had a hand in the creation of one of America's first railroads—the Chesapeake & Ohio (C&O).

As a young man, Washington did surveys for the canal system that was eventually constructed from Virginia to the Ohio

At left: **A CSX diesel, with the silhouette of the kitten 'Chessie' as its logo.**
Below: **A Chessie System freight diesel enters a tunnel in Kentucky.**

River by the James River Company. James River—organized to build a canal system in 1785—included Washington among its charter shareholders to boost subscriptions to the project and gave him 100 shares of stock. He in turn later gave the shares to a local university.

James River continued to operate until 1880, when it was acquired by the Richmond & Allegheny Railroad. Later, the Chesapeake & Ohio, which was chartered in 1868 as a railroad company, took over the Richmond & Allegheny while expanding its empire. Today the old C&O tracks form the backbone of the modern Chessie system (which merged in 1973 with the old Baltimore & Ohio Railroad).

The name 'Chessie' is derived from a mascot—a cat named Chessie—and the cat's name and likeness are still used today as trademarks on the company's locomotives and freight cars. When the Chessie operated passenger trains, its logo was 'Sleep like a kitten.'

The C&O began life as the Louise Railroad, chartered in 1836 and renamed the Virginia Central Railroad in 1850. One of Southern Pacific's 'Big Four,' Collis P Huntington, became associated with the railroad in the late 1860s when Virginia and West Virginia lawmakers passed legislation to rebuild the line from 'the waters of the Chesapeake to the Ohio River.' Huntington, occupied at the time with construction of the Central Pacific Railroad, was assigned the task of building the project.

Despite Huntington's participation and financial support, however, the C&O went bankrupt in 1873. Five years later, Huntington organized a syndicate of investors and brought the line out of bankruptcy, renaming it the Chesapeake & Ohio Railway Co. Under Huntington's new ownership the railroad prospered and expanded to the Virginia coast. It was in this period that the system picked up the James River Company and merged it into its empire.

Huntington extended C&O rails north to Washington, west to Louisville and Dayton and on to Chicago and the Great Lakes. The C&O then served some of the nation's largest and richest coal fields.

The line operated large car building and repair shops and ran a 50,000-car merchandise freight fleet.The Chessie's trackage exceeded 5000 miles in the 1950s, and it acquired control of the historic Baltimore & Ohio in 1972. However, it began to suffer when the automobile industry declined in the late 1970s and the early 1980s.

Baltimore & Ohio

Until its merger with the C&O in the early 1970s, the Baltimore & Ohio (B&O) was one of America's most historic railroads, credited with a number of 'firsts' in its long service on the eastern seaboard and in the Ohio Valley.

The B&O was the first common carrier chartered in the United States and the first to construct tracks for the purpose

Below: These Chesapeake & Ohio 2–6–6–6 locos produced the highest power rating of any steam locomotives, and were used to haul coal trains through the West Virginia mountains. *Above right:* A C&O steam turbine electric. *Below right:* The *Atlantic,* an early Baltimore & Ohio locomotive.

of carrying passengers and freight. Maryland state lawmakers chartered it in 1827, with construction getting under way a year later in 1828.

The idea of building the railroad had been advanced by Philip E Thomas and George Brown after the two had traveled to England to investigate that nation's infant railroad industry. They returned and persuaded fellow businessmen that steam locomotives could be used to haul freight faster than steamboats. The state of Maryland, believing that the two could succeed with their railroad, gave them $500,000; the city of Baltimore also heavily subscribed.

The early B&O featured three different kinds of track, including strap-iron rails laid on wood rails and 'sleepers' or crossties. Its first train was dubbed *The Flying Dutchman* because the train was powered by a horse walking on a treadmill attached to the wheels. It took about an hour and a half to travel 13 miles.

The B&O next experimented with a car driven by a windsail. The Carolina Canal & Railroad company had already proven that wind could be used to drive rail cars, but something more powerful and reliable was needed than horses or wind. The wind-driven car could reach speeds of up to 14 miles per hour, according to a newspaper account of the day, but the push to find a steady source of locomotion continued.

Within five years, the B&O had 135 miles of track. The first rail of this historic line was laid by Charles Carroll, who at the time was the only still-living signer of the Declaration of Independence. It was said of Carroll: 'One man's life formed the connecting link between the political revolution of the last century and the industrial revolution of the present.'

Following construction of the original B&O, work began on other roads. A South Carolina line, the Charleston & Hamburg, was chartered in 1829, and by 1834 it featured 137 miles of tracks. For a short time, the Charleston & Hamburg boasted the longest line under one management. This trackage later became absorbed into the Chessie and then the Seaboard System.

The B&O was one of the more innovative railroads in the United States. The company began using locomotives in the 1830s following experiments conducted by inventor Peter Cooper and Ross Winans, an engineer for the B&O at the time.

Cooper called his small engine *The Tom Thumb* because it weighed just under a ton, small even for a locomotive of its day and age—compared to larger locomotives constructed by the English. Despite its diminutive size, it succeeded in pulling a four-and-a-half ton load around curves and up slight inclines at speeds of up to 15 miles per hour.

The Tom Thumb demonstrated that steam locomotives could be used to replace horses and carriages on American railroads.

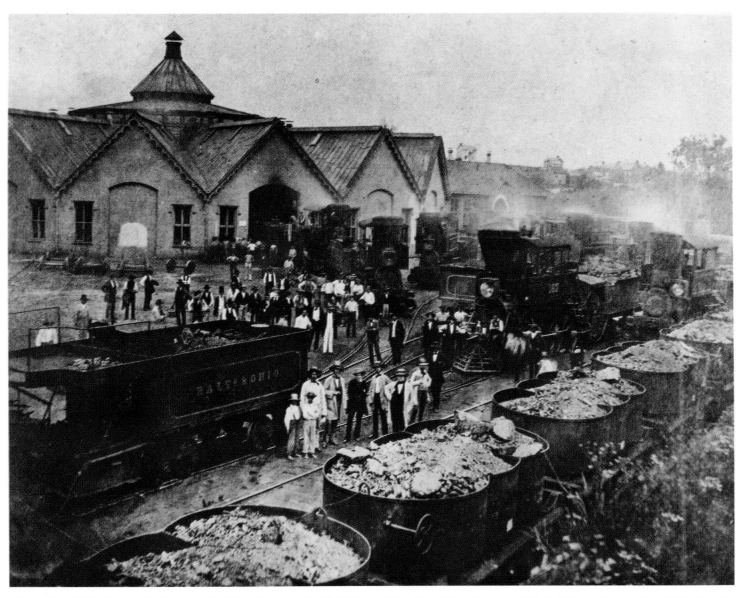

Above: The B&O's shops at Martinsburg, West Virginia during the Civil War. Note the Camelback locomotives and, in the foreground, 'iron pot' coal cars. Stonewall Jackson raided this yard, destroyed 42 locomotives and stole 14.

Below: The *William Mason*, a B&O 4–4–0 wood burner, circa 1850. *Opposite:* Guys and dolls, and a conductor: This classic mid-1940s photo of servicemen and young ladies was taken inside a B&O passenger coach. Rail travel was 'big.'

It had one upright steam cylinder and boiler made from gun barrels, while a revolving fan created a fire draft. On its first run *The Tom Thumb* pushed a train loaded with 23 passengers. Later it raced a horse-drawn car—and lost. It came in second best because the belt that drove the fan flew off its pulley.

The Tom Thumb made Cooper famous in the industrial age, with his locomotive credited as the first steam locomotive built in the United States. The son of an unsuccessful businessman in New York, Cooper succeeded in making money through his inventions. After his experiments with *The Tom Thumb*, Cooper became president of the company that enabled Cyrus K Field to lay the first transcontinental telegraph cable—and later became president of the American Telephone Company.

The success of *The Tom Thumb* set in motion a series of rapid advancements in steam locomotives by other inventors and builders in the United States, so that within a few years, steam locomotives were being produced by the dozens.

The earliest locomotives built for service rather than experimentation were constructed at the West Point Foundry Works in New York City. The first—designated No 1 by the company and called *The Best Friend*—was constructed in 1830 and was put in service on the Charleston & Hamburg Railroad. The next year, *The West Point* was delivered to the same company, and the following year a third locomotive, *The DeWitt Clinton*, was put into use on the Mohawk & Hudson Railroad between Albany and Schenectady.

With the success of these locomotives, machinists in Baltimore, New York and other cities experimented with various engine designs and applications. Within a few years, American builders demonstrated that they could construct suitable locomotives for American terrain and conditions—steep grades and sharp curves.

It was during this period that Matthias Baldwin—whose name would become intertwined with the development and history of steam locomotives—began his career as a locomotive builder when he built his first engine, *The Old Ironsides*, in 1832. By the end of the century, the Baldwin Locomotive Works in Philadelphia was constructing as many as 2700 steam locomotives each year.

The original steam locomotive was the invention of Englishman George Stephenson, and the impact of his celebrated machine, *The Rocket*, was soon felt in the United States. Americans first tried to import Stephenson's design, but they soon came to rely on their own ingenuity. The first American designs constructed for actual service weighed three to five tons, while English versions were twice that.

However, even American models proved too heavy for tracks made of wood covered with strap iron. For example, *The John Bull*, imported from England in 1831 by the Camden and Amboy line, and connecting New York and Philadelphia, weighed 10 tons and was the heaviest locomotive of its time.

After the first few years, practically all American locomotives had eight wheels—four driving wheels under the rear part of the engine and a four-wheel truck carrying the front part of the boiler. The truck was fastened to the engine in such a way that it enabled it to swing or swivel several degrees and enabled the engine and the cars, which employed the 'truck' as well, to round sharp curves without derailing. It was an advancement first used under a passenger coach by Ross Winans of Baltimore in 1831. The same year, he placed the truck under the forward part of a locomotive. Winans' prototype passenger coach car, built for the B&O, was *The Columbia* and served as the passenger car design for many years to come. It featured a central corridor and open platforms on the outside. In 1843 he

was asked to design cars for a railroad under construction between Moscow and St Petersburg.

For many years, Winans' name was associated with the B&O. He had become interested in railroading when he visited the B&O in 1828 to sell horses to the line. Although self-taught in mechanics, he was responsible for a number of the designs and improvements of the early age of railroading.

For example, Winans is credited with the invention of what he called 'friction wheels.' The wheels were fitted firmly to the axles, which were projected into outside bearings called 'journal boxes.' The lids to the boxes could be raised so that the axles could be lubricated.

In 1832 Winans designed an engine called *The Samson*—which was equipped with guiding trucks—for the Baltimore and Susquehanna Railroad. He later formed a company called Gillingham and Winans, which was put in charge of the B&O's Mount Clare shop. In 1844, Winans set up shop to build vertical 0–8–0 locomotives, commonly called 'mud-diggers' because of their tendency to pound clay up from between the ties in wet weather. They were based on European designs.

Winans also experimented with a line of locomotives known as *Camels* or *Camelbacks*. These 0–8–0 engines, unlike the mud diggers, did not have gears. They were distinctive in appearance, with a cab straddling the steam boiler rather than placed at the end.

First manufactured in 1848, this weight-emphasis, located over the driving wheels, made them odd-looking but powerful. *Camelbacks* could haul heavy loads and mastered the B&O's notorious '17-mile grade' which rose 2000 feet. About 200 *Camelbacks* were manufactured and sold by Winans to various railroad lines.

When the B&O attempted to phase out the *Camel* design in the late 1850s, he refused to go along with their decision. He wrote a pamphlet defending the design, but the B&O counterattacked. As a result, Winans lost B&O's business for new locomotives.

When General Stonewall Jackson raided the B&O's Martinsburg, Virginia yards during the Civil War, he destroyed 42 locomotives and commandeered 14 for his army to use in the South. When the B&O attempted to purchase three *Camelback* locomotives which they knew were in Winans' shop to staunch their losses in the raid, Winans bitterly refused to sell. This severed completely his connection with the B&O, though the railroad continued to use the *Camel* design until 1893 when the last one was phased out. Winans himself died in 1877.

The *American* or *Campbell* type is the name applied to many locomotives of the 19th century having four connected driving-wheels and a four-wheel truck. The first engine of this type was constructed in 1836 by James Brooks for Henry R Campbell of Philadelphia. This became the prevailing design for passenger service and remained the dominant form of passenger locomotive through the end of the century.

One essential feature of the modern locomotive awaited introduction until 1837; that was the use of equalizing beams—by means of which the weight upon the driving wheels ceased to be affected by changes in track elevations. All steam locomotives after that date were constructed so that each driving wheel had independent vertical motion; the engine's 'attitude' could change without changing very greatly the pressure imposed by the wheels on the track.

Other developments quickly followed. Differences in design for freight and passenger service quickly evolved in the 1840s. By the turn of the century there were three major types of locomotive—the American-type 4–4–0 locomotive was generally used for passenger service, but more powerful locomotives, with six, eight and 10 driving wheels, were used for hauling freight.

All of this began with *The Tom Thumb*, which operated on B&O tracks. Encouraged by the success of *The Tom Thumb*, B&O officials decided they wanted to see something bigger and better, so they offered to pay $4000 for the best coalburning locomotive design submitted by June of 1831. The locomotive had to weigh less than 3.5 tons and be able to pull a 15-ton load at 15 miles an hour.

Only four entries were received, three of them by watchmakers, one of whom, Phineas Davis, formed a partnership with a machinist and built a four-wheel upright-boiler engine, *The York*—named for York, Pennsylvania. *The York* won the B&O prize.

It weighed about 8000 pounds and ran twice as fast as the B&O required: 30 miles per hour. In the interest of safety, the B&O wanted the boiler pressure to remain at less than 50 pounds per square inch. *The York* could take curves at 15 miles per hour and within a year was making regular passenger runs. The firm of Davis & Gartner built two more locomotives before Davis was killed in a railroad accident.

Before his death, Davis became B&O's master mechanic. His second locomotive design, called *The Atlantic*, was the prototype for *The Grasshopper* class of engine used for many years by the B&O. These vertical boiler locomotives were used right up to the turn of the century.

The name *Grasshopper* was derived from the drive mechanism on the locomotive, which consisted of overhead walking beams and long rods that turned on a pair of cranks on countershafts. The motion of the beams and rods reminded railroad employees of the leg motion of grasshoppers.

The Baltimore & Ohio was associated in its early history with more than just the development of railroad equipment. In 1843, Samuel F B Morse—the inventor of the telegraph—strung wire along B&O's right of way to test his magnetic telegraph. Morse installed two telegraph keys in one of B&O's Baltimore stations and sent the world's first electronic message: 'What hath God wrought?' Later the telegraph became closely associated with the growth and development of the railroad.

The B&O often found itself in the very heart of Civil War fighting, sustaining much damage while it transported troops to

Above: Ellicot City Station, 13 miles from Baltimore, was the first terminus of the B&O. *Below opposite:* A Seaboard System freight crosses Virginia's Copper Creek Bridge. *Above right:* This Western Maryland diesel, with the WM neat yellow pinstripe paintjob, resides at the B&O Museum in Baltimore.

and from the battlefields. When the Civil War ended, the B&O extended its tracks to Pittsburgh and Chicago, aquiring steamboats, docks and grain elevators in the process, including a dry dock in Baltimore, vacation hotels in the mountains and express and sleeping car manufacturing companies. The company built huge terminals in Chicago, St Louis and Philadelphia.

The B&O came out second best, however, when it went up against the Pennsylvania Railroad for control of the Wilmington, Baltimore & Washington Railroad (WBW). When the 'Pennsy' won the battle, it refused to allow B&O trains to use the WBW's tracks to reach New York City.

The B&O retaliated, refusing permission for the Pennsy to enter Philadelphia by way of the Schuylkill East Side Terminal. When the nationwide financial panic of 1873 struck, the heavy expenses associated with its quarrel with the Pennsy threw the B&O into bankruptcy. But the courts allowed the railroad to borrow money, and officials were able to nurse the line back to financial health in 1895.

The B&O lays claim to many 'firsts' in American railroading. It was the first line to earn money by carrying passengers, the first to use car wheels that revolved with their axles, and the first to operate an eight-wheeled passenger coach.

It was the first railroad to publish and issue timetables and the first to use iron boxcars. In 1932, five years after the B&O celebrated its 100th anniversary, the Columbia Broadcasting System made the first radio broadcast from a moving train operated by the B&O between Baltimore and Washington.

Western Maryland

The Western Maryland (WM) Railroad was often called 'the Mason and Dixon Line' because it served the territory along the imaginary line separating the North and South. The Western Maryland was chartered in 1852, but construction was held up for 10 years for lack of financing. In 1863 the Union Army commandeered the Western Maryland to transport troops and supplies for the Battle of Gettysburg. When the fighting was over and the Confederate forces had been

repelled, the Western Maryland was used to haul dead and injured men away from the battlefield.

Five months later, the WM also carried Abraham Lincoln to the battlefield, where he gave one of the most famous speeches in history—the Gettysburg Address.

The Western Maryland prospered after the war by aquiring and merging with other lines, then became part of the Chessie System in 1972. Most recently, the Western Maryland has relied on coal hauling for most of its revenue.

Chicago, South Shore & South Bend Railroad

The Chicago, South Shore & South Bend Railroad (CSSSB) continues to operate commuter service in the Chicago metropolitan region and provides some freight service. It is a relatively young railroad, having started in 1901 as the Chicago and Indiana Air Line Railway. Samuel Insull, who took control of the line in 1925, departed in 1932 when the system went bankrupt, but not before Insull had modernized the CSSSB by upgrading its electrification system and purchasing more modern cars. The C&O bought the line in 1967.

Seaboard Coast Line

The Seaboard Coast Line traces its beginning back to North Carolina in the 1830s when one of its two parent companies boasted the longest continuous track of railroad in the world. Today it boasts another record. The Seaboard operates the longest stretch of straight track in the United States—its 78.8-mile stretch between Hamlet and Wilmington.

The various lines that have disappeared within the Seaboard Coast have similar histories. The first of these was known as the Petersburg Railroad, chartered by the state of Virginia in 1830. The Petersburg featured a line extending north from the Roanoke River near Weldon, North Carolina to the Virginia state line. From there the road consisted of strap-iron rails fastened to yellow-pine stringers supported by oak crossties. Eventually this line became known as the Atlantic Coast Railroad.

Farther east, work had begun on a separate line known as the Portsmouth & Roanoke, the parent of the Seaboard Air

Line Railway, which was chartered in 1832. Its first train ran four years later when track laying was completed.

After receiving its charter in 1834, work started on a third railroad known as the Wilmington & Raleigh; later it became known as the Wilmington & Weldon. Organizers began laying track across the eastern half of North Carolina, but lack of money delayed construction until 1836, and the final spike of the 162-mile track—America's longest continuous line at the time—was driven near Rocky Mount in 1840.

Still another ancestor of the Seaboard was the Richmond & Petersburg Railroad, which ran between Richmond and Pocahontas on the north bank of the Appomattox River opposite Petersburg. There were other early lines that now make up the Seaboard, but the name itself first appeared in 1846 when the Richmond & St Petersburg became the Seaboard &

Above: A Seaboard passenger train near Ducktown, Tennessee. *At right*: The Louisville & Nashville's *Hummingbird* passenger train. *Above right:* B&O and Chessie locos in Grafton, West Virginia. *At left:* Chessie, Seaboard and Southern lines locomotives at the triple crossing in Richmond, Virginia.

Roanoke. Probably the first use of the name Seaboard Air Line was in 1873 when an agency by that name was established near Portsmouth.

The Atlantic Coast Line began to take shape following the Civil War when a Baltimore capitalist merged four railroads together to form the Seaboard Coast Line—so named because the system paralleled the Atlantic Ocean.

After first reaching South Carolina during the 1890s, the Atlantic Coast Line extended into Florida in 1900. Later the system was expanded into Georgia and other southern states. The merger of the Atlantic Coast and the Seaboard Railroad into the Seaboard Coast Line Railroad took place in 1967. On 24 September 1980, Seaboard Coast Line Industries merged with the Chessie System.

Louisville & Nashville

The Louisville & Nashville—affectionately called the L&N for more than 125 years—was chartered in 1850 by the Commonwealth of Kentucky. It was organized to meet the need for transportation between Louisville on the Ohio River and Nashville.

Despite opposition from steamboat and stagecoach interests, construction was given an official stamp of approval when the Tennessee state legislature authorized the building of a line from Nashville towards Louisville.

While construction moved southward, trains began operating on the completed track. When the L&N's first train made its run in 1855, it was forced to stop three times, once for water and twice so that cows could be driven off the track. The train never traveled faster than 15 miles per hour, and could only travel eight miles, anyway, to the end of the tracks. It would be another four years before trains could travel all the way between the two charter cities, a distance of 187 miles.

When the link between Nashville and Louisville was made, the L&N began operating with 18 wood-burning locomotives and less than 100 passenger and freight cars. By the time the Civil War began in 1861, the little railroad had 269 miles of track—small compared to larger lines in the northeast.

Because Kentucky was a so-called 'Border State,' the L&N was forced to serve two armies, the Union soldiers and the Confederates. But most freight traffic on the L&N line in Tennessee was carried for the Confederates. Eventually, managers from the Union side assumed control of the line, but not before several battles to obtain control of the railroad had been fought. As the Union soldiers moved south, the Confederate troops did considerable damage to the railroad. By the end of the war, more than half the rolling stock had been destroyed in fighting—but the L&N itself was in sound financial condition.

During the Reconstruction Era the L&N began a program to expand, and within a period of 30 years, lines were extended into Memphis, St Louis, Cincinnati, Birmingham and along the Gulf Coast including New Orleans.

With L&N's entrance into the Gulf port cities of Mobile, Pensacola and New Orleans in the early 1880s, the heretofore regional line was able to extend its horizons overseas. It could now provide international markets for the agricultural and material goods produced by its customers in the major cities served by the railroad.

For many years the L&N was known as 'the railroad that carried coal,' and between 1879 and 1881 the line gained access to the coal fields of western Kentucky by purchasing various trackage. Fifty-six railroads, mostly short lines, were bought, leased or constructed in that period.

The L&N continued its expansion, acquiring the Kentucky Central in 1891 and making further acquisitions in 1909 and 1910, as well as constructing more than 100 miles of track through the coal fields of eastern Kentucky. This proved an important source of revenue for the line, especially during the two world wars. Other mergers occurred in the 1950s, 1960s and 1970s.

By the time the L&N merged with the Seaboard system, it operated more than 6570 miles of track in 13 states in the southeastern section of the United States. For many years, the Louisville & Nashville was known as 'the Old Reliable' and was the second-ranking member of the Seaboard Coast Lines.

The L&N operated *The Pan American*, an all-Pullman express train between Cincinnati and New Orleans. The run was widely known because its sounds were broadcast by radio during the 1930s and 1940s. In 1940, the L&N began operating *The South Wind* and *The Dixie Flyer* between Chicago and Miami.

The South Wind used a heavy, Pacific-type locomotive coupled to a supertank with a capacity of 27.5 tons of coal and 20,000 gallons of water. With this advantage in terms of fuel and water, she was able to make the 205-mile run without a stop—which remains a record today for steam locomotives.

The L&N was one of the more successful passenger railroads in the 1940s, but with the arrival of the passenger jet and the personal automobile, traffic declined rapidly. In 1950, for example, the railroad carried 2.6 million passengers. Since then the L&N has cut the number of its passenger trains from 74 to 34. In 1971, passenger service was turned over to Amtrack.

Because of its access to cheap bituminous coal in Kentucky and Tennessee, the L&N was one of the last holdouts against the diesel locomotive. It did not buy its first diesels for freight service until 1950, long after other railroads had converted from steam to diesel. In 1957, the L&N finally scrapped its last 36 steam locomotives and became fully dieselized.

The Clinchfield

The Clinchfield Railroad began in 1831 when organizers wanted to build a wagon road from Elkhorn City, Kentucky to Spartanburg, South Carolina. At the time, no less than 18 companies were organized to build railroads, including the Charleston, Cincinatti & Chicago (CC&C). But they all failed, until the project was revived and completed in 1912.

The story of how the Clinchfield was finally built is one of the more interesting sagas of eastern railroading. Organizers wanted to build a railroad from Charleston, South Carolina to Ashland, Kentucky to tap the large coal deposits in eastern Kentucky as well as the iron ore deposits near Cranberry, North Carolina. But the firm underwriting the project went bankrupt before it could get the tracks built.

Several sales and reorganizations were conducted before progress could be made. In each state, four corporations were formed to take over the line in that state. But this arrangement did not work either. By 1908, however, the project began to stabilize, and by 1980 more than 80 miles of track had been constructed.

The Clinchfield serves as a bridge between the Atlantic Seaboard and the Great Lakes. For many years, the great challenge was to bridge the Cumberland and Blue Ridge mountains with a rail system. When completed, the line consisted of two long tunnels, 53 shorter ones and five miles of bridges and viaducts. Before it became part of the CSX Corporation it was leased to the L&N and the Atlantic Seaboard.

When the Clinchfield was finally constructed, it served as a showcase for modern railroad construction, although the roadbed gave the engineers who surveyed and planned it a raft of problems. Instead of seeking low grades by going around the mountains of Appalachia, as other lines had done, Clinchfield used tunnels and cut-and-fill construction to skirt the rugged landscape.

One of the largest tunnels along the line was the 7854-foot passage through Sanday Ridge between Virginia and Kentucky. At the Blue Ridge side, workmen carved out a 4135-foot tunnel. More than 10 miles of the system consists of tunnels, while another five miles is bridges and viaducts.

The cut-and-fill construction required moving up to 25 million cubic yards of earth, but the result was one of the best railroad beds in the eastern United States. The opening of the Clinchfield allowed the coal fields—consisting of several hundred thousand acres of thick-seamed bituminous coal in southwestern Virginia and eastern Kentucky—to be tapped. However, the line never reached Ashland; the builders brought the system to an end at Elkhorn City. Nevertheless it proved to be a profitable line because of its location and access to cheap coal.

When the Clinchfield began operating in 1880, it deployed just six steam locomotives and just under 270 freight cars. At the time the system was leased to the L&N in 1925, the equipment had grown to 96 locomotives and more than 7700 pieces of rolling stock.

In the age of steam, the system used smaller freight and passenger steam locomotives. Among the engines in its roundhouses were *Pacifics*, *Mikados* and *Mallets*, with three different wheel arrangements: 2–6–6–2, 2–8–8–2 and 4–6–6–4. The C-class, or 600-series *Mallets*, were among the finest steam engines used on any system. But the Clinchfield deployed 10 diesel locomotives. By 1955 —the same year that passenger trains stopped operating on the Clinchfield—all steam had disappeared.

The Clinchfield became part of the Family Lines System when the Atlantic Coast Line and the Louisville & Nashville leased the properties of the Carolina, Clinchfield & Ohio for 99 years. The name was then reorganized as the Clinchfield Railroad Company.

Georgia Railroad

The Georgia Railroad, one of the original Family Lines companies, was one of the few railroads in the US to issue its own currency. In fact, the railroad was originally tied to a bank when it first got its charter. The Georgia was chartered in late December 1833 as the Central Rail Road & Banking Co of Georgia and was the first railroad to operate in the state when *The Florida*, an American-type 4–4–0, hauled a passenger train from Madison to Atlanta.

The Georgia prospered in the days before the Civil War, but suffered greatly at the hands of Union General William T Sherman during his 'March to the Sea.' Sherman's men wrecked more than 60 miles of the railroad track, burned depots and destroyed bridges, and left the roundhouse and railroad yards at Atlanta in disrepair.

The railroad was fortunate in that its managers were able to operate the company during the fighting—and still make a profit. But the profits evaporated after the war because the currency was no longer valid.

Amazingly, the Georgia was able to transport more than 100,000 Confederate veterans back to their home towns after the war, and to do so without charge to the men.

When hostilities were over, the Georgia acquired the Atlanta & West Point Railroad and became co-owner of the Western Railway of Alabama. In 1881, the three systems were leased to Colonel William M Wadley for 99 years, and the banking company was separated from the railroad.

Wadley, who was also president of the bank, assigned half of his interest in the properties to the L&N Railroad and the other half the to the Central Railroad. Eventually, the three lines were leased to the L&N and then became part of the Family Lines System.

South Carolina Railroad

The South Carolina system was built mostly with slave labor hired from plantations and before the Civil War became one of the most profitable railroad systems in the South. For example, profits before 1861 totaled more than $1.5 million. Prosperity continued for the first three years of the war when gross receipts totaled more than $6 million, allowing managers to return a 16 percent dividend to shareholders. The money, however, paid in Confederate dollars, later became worthless.

But prosperity ended when Sherman marched through the South and destroyed everything in his path that could be used by the enemy. When Sherman and his soldiers were finished, the system counted four locomotives, five passenger cars and 36 freight cars—none in good shape and all needing repair.

The Civil War

The Civil War was the first major conflict in which railroads played a significant part in the fighting. At the outset, the North possessed more than 22,000 miles of track while the

Above: An Atlantic Coast line 4–8–4 steam locomotive, built by Baldwin. *Overleaf:* A CSX diesel doubleheader emerges from a tunnel, and a CSX 'piggyback' freight loaded with truck trailers passes over the tunnel in Louisville, Kentucky. Piggybacking facilitates fast freight movement.

South had just 9000. The North's advantage included ownership of foundries and locomotive factories. The North had dozens scattered well away from the fighting, while the South had just one, in Richmond, Virginia.

Many of the predecessors of today's CSX Corp were caught in the thick of the fighting. One of the first incidents came in 1861 when Confederate General Stonewall Jackson raided the Baltimore & Ohio yards at Martinsburg, Virginia, destroyed 42 locomotives, and carried another 14 back to the South.

One of the greatest engineers of the war, General Herman Haupt, was responsible for keeping Union railroads operating during many battles. After several early Confederate victories, the US War Department used Haupt to get damaged track repaired and the trains moving again.

A graduate of West Point when he was 18, he resigned a year later to become a railroad engineer and spent his early career locating routes for railroads. Because written engineering books on railroad construction were in short supply, he wrote the definitive text on the subject: *General Theory of Bridge Construction.* It became a standard text in the United States as well as Europe and the rest of the world.

The Union Army used his expertise to repair track and bridges so that the North could take Richmond, the capitol of the South, and end the war. Although the strategy failed in the early years of the war, Haupt was not to blame. He and his men performed heroically under battlefield conditions. Using inexperienced soldiers as bridge workers, he reconstructed the Potomac Creek Bridge in nine days, taking anything that he could find for materials.

When President Lincoln visited the bridge site, he wrote, 'I have seen the most remarkable structure that human eyes have ever rest upon. That man Haupt has built a bridge 400 feet long and nearly 100 feet high, and upon my word, gentlemen, there is nothing in it but beanpoles and cornstalks.'

The Confederates won one of their greatest Civil War battles in 1861 when they eluded Union forces assigned to watch them and rode the Manassas Gap Railroad across the Blue

Above: This CSX freight will probably not back up, so it's time to get off the railroad bridge at Frankfurt, Kentucky. *Above right:* Seaboard (left) and Chessie (right) locomotives are positioned to meet, at Chessie's ultramodern Queensgate Yard in Cincinnati, Ohio. Note the switching tower behind them.

Ridge Mountains to Bull Run, which turned the tide in their favor. Later, when Confederate forces attempted to storm Washington, they were met by Union troops who had also traveled to the battlefront aboard the Manassas Gap. (Haupt's men rebuilt five bridges, spanning from 60 to 120 feet, *in one day.* Before the war ended, the Bull Run bridge had been rebuilt seven times.)

Haupt, who in 1862 was promoted to brigadier general for his work, commanded railroad construction and transportation projects for a dozen other battles involving Union troops. Haupt's corps of bridge builders could also be destructive when they had to be.

They played major roles in General Sherman's march through Georgia. Haupt's men stoked the fireboxes of Confederate locomotives without water in the boilers and watched them explode. Then they tore rails from the tracks, heated them up and twisted them around trees so they could not be reused by southern forces. The twisted rails were known as 'Sherman's neckties.'

The West Point Route

The West Point Route consists of two short lines, the Atlanta & West Point Rail and the Western Railway of Alabama. The Atlanta & West Point began as the Atlanta & LaGrange Rail Road in 1849. It was completed in 1854 and eventually became part of the Georgia Railroad.

The Atlanta & West Point prospered in the decade before the Civil War. By the end of 1859, its profits from the capital invested in it was 17 percent. But the profits plummeted with the arrival of the war.

The line played a major role in the transport of Confederate troops and supplies right up to 1864, when Union troops seized Atlanta. As the city fell, federal troops destroyed some 18 miles of the A&WP tracks along with a number of depots, bridges, water stations and other property.

The Western Railway of Alabama began in 1832 as the Montgomery Railroad, but had to struggle since only 32 miles of track were laid from Montgomery to Franklin. After a bankruptcy and sale, the line emerged as the Montgomery & West Point Rail Road. The track was extended to West Point, Georgia in 1851.

The road then began to prosper, carrying bales of cotton to shipping points until the Civil War started. Then, instead of cotton, it carried passengers. In 1863, it carried a record 268,000 passengers—200,000 of them Confederate soldiers—to and from the battlefields.

In 1864 the line suffered at the hands of advancing Union troops. Much of its track was destroyed and equipment and buildings were burned at several locations. The system was substantially reconstructed after the war, but it never recovered financially.

In 1870 it was reorganized as the Western Railroad of Alabama, and in 1875 the property was sold to the Georgia Railroad. Later its name was changed to the Western Railway of Alabama.

The CSX Routes

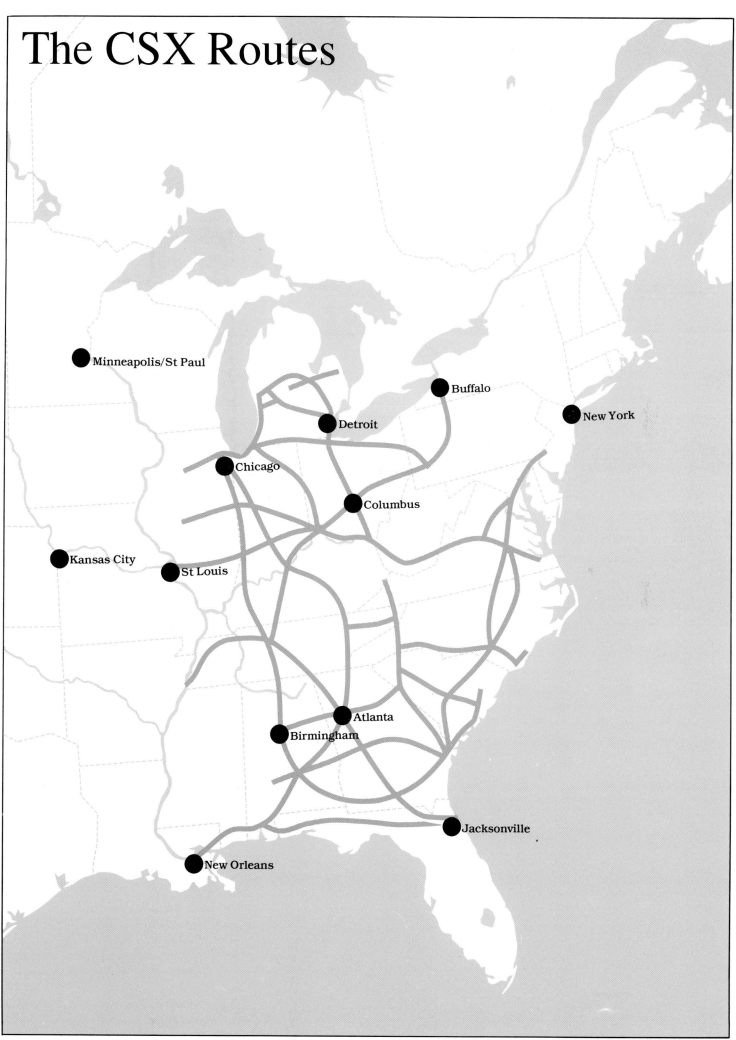

CONRAIL

Created by an Act of Congress

The rise and fall of America's eastern railroads is mirrored in the story of Conrail—the Consolidated Railroad Corporation. Congress created the Conrail line in 1970 in response to the collapse of the Penn Central—the largest corporate bankruptcy ever filed up to that time in US history. Penn Central had been created just two years earlier with the merger of the Pennsylvania, the New York Central and the New York, New Haven & Hartford railroads.

Later, Conrail expanded its scope of operation with the passage of the Rail Revitalization and Regulatory Reform Act of 1975, which designated Conrail to take over the remnants of a number of bankrupt eastern railroads, including the Central of New Jersey, the Erie Lackawanna, the Lehigh & Hudson River, the Lehigh Valley, the Penn Central, the Reading and the Pennsylvania-Reading Seashores lines, many of which trace their histories to the very beginnings of the American railroad system.

In the 1970s Conrail sold its so-called 'Northeast Corridor' lines—connecting Boston, New York, Washington, Philadelphia and Harrisburg—to Amtrak, the national passenger train service operated by the US government. Conrail also sold or abandoned thousands of miles of other track. In 1981 Congress authorized Conrail to give away or sell many commuter services under its jurisdiction to state, local and regional agencies.

When Conrail took over ailing Penn Central, Congress allotted $2 billion in subsidies to keep the trains rolling. Conrail had expected to turn a profit in the late 1970s, but due to the expense of repairing, replacing or rebuilding roadbed and rolling stock, it failed to do so. Since 1981, however, Conrail has been more successful.

In the mid 1980s, revenues exceeded $3 billion and operating income approached $400 million. Having returned to profitability, Conrail was also returned to publicly held ownership in 1987 when its stock was traded on major US exchanges.

Philadelphia-based Conrail is the nation's sixth largest railroad, with more than 14,000 miles of track and more than 36,000 employees. It serves 15 states in the east and midwest as well as the District of Columbia and Montreal and is the largest automotive and intermodal transportation company in North America, serving seven of the 10 top consumer markets in the nation.

New York Central

The New York Central Company—one of the two major backbones of Conrail—was one of the premier systems of the late 19th and early 20th centuries. However, like many of its competitors in the northeast, it fell into disrepair in the 1950s and 1960s. Despite a merger with the Pennsylvania Railroad in 1968, the NYC continued to hemmorhage red ink, placing it beyond the salvation of even its best managers.

Opposite: Conrail diesel (near) and electric locomotives in Kearny, New Jersey. *Below:* This Mercury adorned the NYC's Grand Central Station.

The New York Central (NYC) began in the 1820s not as one railroad, but as 10 small lines. The oldest, the Mohawk & Hudson Railroad, was chartered in 1826, but opened in 1831, operating the 17 miles between Albany and Schenectady in New York to connect the Hudson River with the Erie Canal. Originally, it was intended to be a horse-drawn line, but directors decided to try the new steam locomotives then under development.

The first locomotive, *The DeWitt Clinton*, had the distinction of being the third locomotive built in the US by David Matthew, who constructed the locomotive at his West Point Foundry in New York City. *The DeWitt Clinton*, featuring four large wheels driven by a 10-horsepower engine, and capable of achieving speeds as high as 30 miles per hour, was primitive compared to those machines that evolved in later years.

Matthew claimed a number of firsts in the development of America's railroads, including the roundhouse, the snow plow, the spark arrester, the locomotive cab, the geared turntable and a steam preheater in the tender.

The success of the Mohawk & Hudson led to the construction of nine lines by nine different companies to connect cities throughout New York state. By 1842, Buffalo was connected to New York, then Boston to Albany, creating a link between the Great Lakes and Boston.

The New York Central emerged in 1853 when the Mohawk & Hudson merged with the nine other railroads, which greatly benefited travelers. The 10 original railroads had never been able to schedule connecting service without delays or missed trains, and travelers were never sure when one train would arrive and another leave.

Shipping magnate Cornelius Vanderbilt began buying into the NYC in the 1860s and within a few years became closely associated with it. He gained control of the NYC in 1870, then merged his Hudson River Railroad with the NYC to create the New York Central & Hudson Railroad. With the merger, service improved, traffic increased and profits soared, and Vanderbilt began to acquire other lines and add them to the

NYC, creating one of the most extensive systems in the country.

Born on Staten Island in 1794, Vanderbilt had descended from Dutch colonial settlers. He started his first business venture at age 16, operating a ferry between Staten Island and Manhattan with a sailboat purchased for less than $100. With the profits, he bought several schooners and used them for coastal trading from Long Island Sound to Charleston, South Carolina.

During the War of 1812, Vanderbilt won contracts to provision forts around New York Harbor. He then sold his business and went to work for a steam navigation company, where he learned enough to start his own steamship line on the Hudson. He demonstrated such skill at cutting fares and gaining new business in the process that his archrival and chief competitor Daniel Drew was forced to sell out to Vanderbilt in a bitterly felt capitulation. Drew would spend years trying to avenge the loss.

Vanderbilt was soon operating ships sailing up and down the Atlantic coast, ranging even as far as Mexico and Central America, and was so successful that he was dubbed 'The Commodore.' His fleet, the American Atlantic & Pacific Ship Canal Company, made him a fortune as it carried thousands of so-called '49ers' across Nicaragua and Panama to California.

Vanderbilt did not enter the railroad business, however, until he was 70 years old, when he purchased stock in the New York & Harlem Railroad. He saw an opportunity to bring the railroad into the heart of New York City and convinced the city council to allow an extension of the line—as street car tracks—all the way to the Battery in lower Manhattan. The decision sent shares in his railroad soaring.

He again encountered his old nemesis, Daniel Drew, who was plotting to destroy Vanderbilt's railroad through stock manipulation. Drew attempted to sell the railroad stock short, but his strategy backfired when he and his co-conspirators were unable to convince the city council to rescind its decision to extend the tracks.

Vanderbilt eventually purchased control of the Hudson River Railroad and petitioned state lawmakers in Albany to merge the Hudson River line with the New York and Harlem. Once again Drew tried to stop Vanderbilt by selling the railroad stock short before Vanderbilt could gain control, but he was again outwitted. Vanderbilt snapped up the stock as it plummeted on the market, forcing Drew to pay dearly for the shares he had shorted.

Not quite ready to give up, however, Drew tried one more time to thwart his old enemy by offering to sell his Hudson River Boat Line to the New York Central so it could transport freight from Albany to New York. Yet before a decision could be made the Hudson froze, forcing Drew to use Vanderbilt's Hudson River Railroad to move his own clients' goods up and down the river. Vanderbilt responded by halting traffic on the east side of the river to prevent Drew's trains from connecting with the New York Central, thus forcing Drew's passengers to trudge across a railroad bridge to catch Vanderbilt's trains waiting on the west side. Vanderbilt defended his actions by saying that New York state law forbade his trains from crossing the Hudson. The law, he was quick to point out, had been enacted at the request of the New York Central to avoid competition.

As the Central's passengers continued walking the two miles across the bridge, the company's stock accordingly dropped, and when it hit $18 a share, Vanderbilt bought it and assumed control of the NYC in 1867. Later, he extended the rails to Chicago to create the basic outline of his transportation empire.

Above left: This New York Central & Hudson River 4–4–0 wood burner, shown here with crew and hangers-on, was built in 1860. *Below:* The Hudson River Terminal in New York City, circa 1870. *Above:* Grand Central Depot on 42nd Street in New York City, circa 1872. Grand Central Station came in 1899.

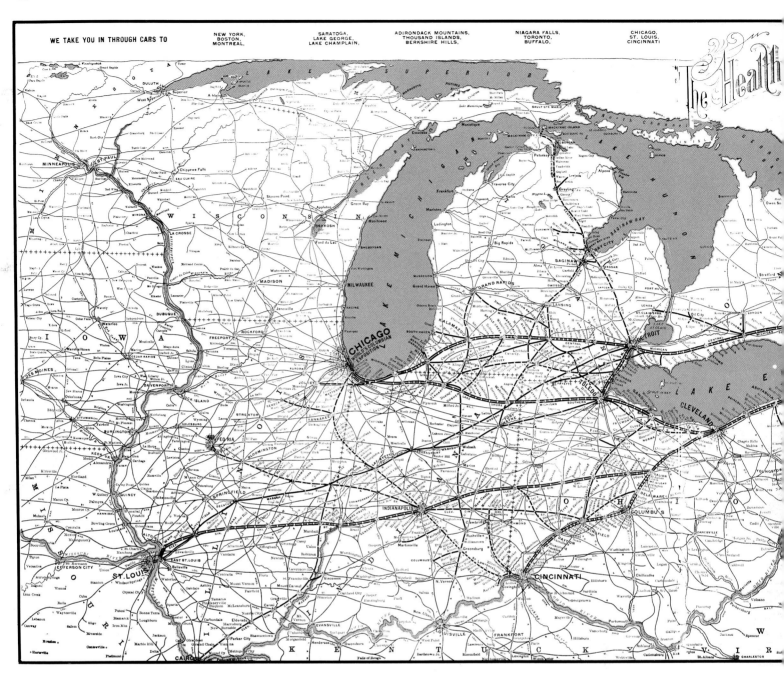

Above: The NYC combined advertising and direction in this 19th century map.
Below, opposite: Railroad baron Cornelius Vanderbilt, aka 'the Commodore.'

Vanderbilt, never satisfied with what he had, pursued other railroads. He tried to gain control of the Erie Railroad in 1868, but was rebuffed by Jay Gould, Jim Fisk and Drew, the three robber barons who then controlled the Erie. However, Vanderbilt was able to add the Lake Shore & Michigan Central Railway and the Canada Southern Railway to his empire in 1873, the same year that he started construction of the cavernous Grand Central Station terminal in Manhattan.

Vanderbilt soon had competition he did not want from other railroads. Barons and would-be barons like Gould, Fisk and Drew would start a nuisance railroad, then try to unload it on competitors at a profit. When Vanderbilt attempted to buy up Erie stock, Gould's printing presses changed $10 million worth of Erie bonds into 100,000 shares of common stock, making it more costly for Vanderbilt to acquire a controlling interest in the Erie. Vanderbilt had permitted the three men to issue the bonds to replace worn rails and lay a third rail to allow standard gauge trains to run on Erie's 6-foot-gauge tracks. Hovering at the edge of bankruptcy because of more

than $7 million in worthless stock, Vanderbilt threatened to sell his worthless shares in the New York Central until the banks loaned him the money he needed to get back his $7 million from the Erie.

When he died in 1885, Vanderbilt's personal fortune was estimated at more than $100 million, making him one of the richest men in the world. At that time, his sons, William Henry (Vanderbilt) and Cornelius II, took control of the NYC.

In the eight years after he took over from his father in 1877, Cornelius was able to increase the family fortune from $100 to $200 million. For instance, he offered secret rebates to major customers to retain their business. The railroad would publish a public rate, but Cornelius offered better rates way below those to major customers such as steel and oil companies, enabling them to save millions of dollars in shipping costs and—more important to the NYC—helping the railroad to survive economic hard times.

Cornelius later sold his stock in the Central to divert negative publicity about his management of the railroad. In 1879, with the help of JP Morgan who got $30 million to make the deal, he sold 250,000 of his 400,000 NYC shares. Morgan joined the NYC board of directors and received a promise that

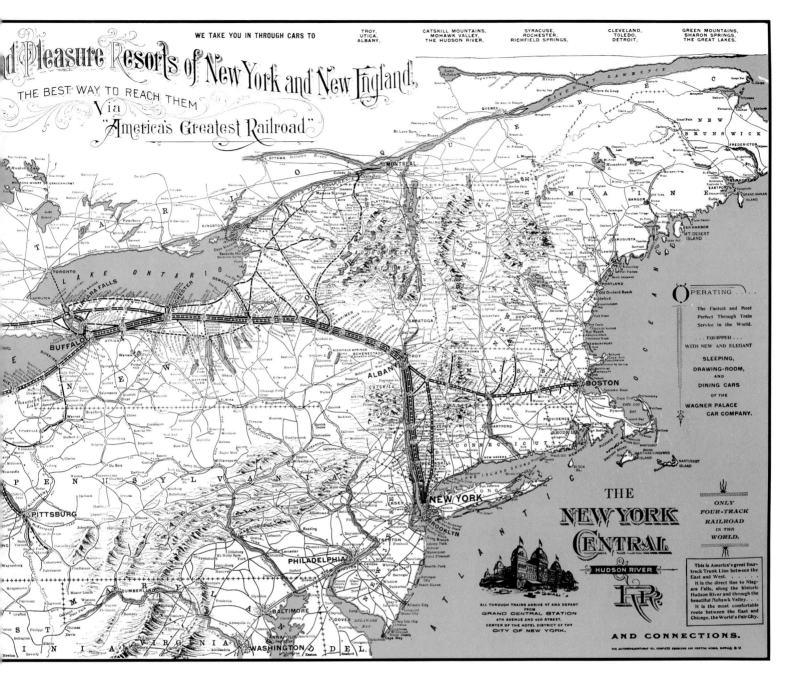

WE TAKE YOU IN THROUGH CARS TO — TROY, UTICA, ALBANY. — CATSKILL MOUNTAINS, MOHAWK VALLEY, THE HUDSON RIVER, — SYRACUSE, ROCHESTER, RICHFIELD SPRINGS, — CLEVELAND, TOLEDO, DETROIT, — GREEN MOUNTAINS, SHARON SPRINGS, THE GREAT LAKES.

d Pleasure Resorts of New York and New England,

THE BEST WAY TO REACH THEM

Via "America's Greatest Railroad"

OPERATING

The Fastest and Most Perfect Through Train Service in the World.

...EQUIPPED...

WITH NEW AND ELEGANT

SLEEPING, DRAWING-ROOM, AND DINING CARS OF THE WAGNER PALACE CAR COMPANY.

THE NEW YORK CENTRAL

HUDSON RIVER

ONLY FOUR-TRACK RAILROAD IN THE WORLD.

This is America's great four-track Trunk Line between the East and West.

It is the direct line to Niagara Falls, along the historic Hudson River and through the beautiful Mohawk Valley.

It is the most comfortable route between the East and Chicago, the World's Fair City.

ALL THROUGH TRAINS ARRIVE AT AND DEPART FROM GRAND CENTRAL STATION 4TH AVENUE AND 42D STREET, CENTER OF THE HOTEL DISTRICT OF THE CITY OF NEW YORK.

AND CONNECTIONS.

the Central would pay at least $8 a share in dividends for at least five years. He was responsible for an agreement between the competing Pennsylvania Railroad and the New York Central in 1885 that allowed the two firms to set rates without fear of competition.

Congress passed the Interstate Railroad Act in 1887 to stop such illegal rate setting, but NYC and other railroads fought vigorously to prevent the government from setting rates itself and were able to maintain high tariffs by cooperating and buying out smaller lines.

By the end of the century, perhaps as a consequence, the NYC controlled 12,000 miles of track and earned in excess of $60 million a year. It had also adopted a slogan, 'The water level route—you can sleep.' It advertised widely for overnight travelers on the basis of its route to Chicago and St Louis which operated on mostly level track.

In 1891, the NYC made a bid to capture the passenger traffic from other carriers with the introduction of an express steam locomotive, No 870. Later, it introduced the American-type 999 and gave it a test run on *The Empire State Express*, achieving speeds in excess of 112 miles per hour. Nothing on rails had traveled so fast before.

In 1896, Cornelius suffered a debilitating illness. Then at the end of the century, William (Henry) turned over his interest in the firm to others. For the next fifty years, through two wars and the Depression of the 1930s, the NYC was considered one of the best run railroads in the United States. By the end of the 1950s, however, the railroad could not resist the economic trends that were draining its capital. As industries shifted from the north to the west and south, drastically reduced freight car loadings dragged the system deeply into debt.

The NYC's misfortunes paralleled the economic histories of the regions it served after World War II. During the boom years of the early 1950s, traffic expanded quickly to meet the demands of the coal, steel and automobile industries.

However, when the interstate highway system was completed in the 1960s, trucks took an increasing amount of freight traffic. Within two years of the opening of the New York thruway in 1954, the New York Central lost more than half of its long-haul passenger traffic. The opening of the St Lawrence Seaway also impacted freight movements to the point that the merger with the Pennsylvania Railroad in 1968 was long overdue. Ironically, though first announced in 1962, it took executives from the Central and the Pennsy six years to get the merger approved by regulatory agencies.

Above: An NYC 4–4–0, *Mariposa.* *Below:* The NYC subsidiary Boston & Albany's locomotive shop. *Right:* A 1946 ad for the NYC's *20th Century Limited.*

The *Magic Carpet* rolls out again

IT'S CENTURY TIME! A minute ago, outside the station, you were in the heart of a great city, with hurrying crowds, blaring taxis, newsboys shouting the evening headlines. Now you're in a different world as you follow that crimson carpet down the platform of Grand Central Terminal toward the softly lighted, streamlined cars that will be your club on wheels for tonight.

Relax by Twilight

Magically, the day's tension vanishes when you step into the Century's luxurious Observation car. Deep cushioned easy chairs invite you to relax. And outside the wide windows, the twilit beauty of the Water Level Route unrolls a background for repose.

The Face is Familiar

Beside superb cuisine and service, there's a fascination about dinner on this favorite train of famous people. For nearby may be a lovely face you last saw in technicolor, or a distinguished one that would be news on any financial page.

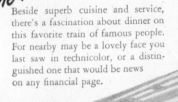

Awake Refreshed

You arrive looking and feeling your best. For all night, in the quiet privacy of your room, a spacious bed, a rubber-foam mattress, and the smooth Water Level Route have conspired to give you deep, refreshing sleep.

NEW YORK CENTRAL

The Water Level Route—You Can Sleep

The *only* all-room extra-fare train between New York and Chicago.

20TH CENTURY LIMITED

The Pennsy

Dubbed 'The Standard Railroad of the World,' the Pennsylvania Railroad was one of the largest and most profitable for many years. The 'Pennsy' took as its company logo the symbol of the state of Pennsylvania—the Keystone—which was originally used in 1877 after the Pennsy and other railroads suffered their first major labor strike.

In the age of steam, the Pennsy was credited with doing more than any other railroad to advance the design and efficiency of steam locomotives. The company created new designs in its own shops and worked closely with the notable builders of the day, including Baldwin, American Locomotive Company, R Norris & Son and Ross Winans. The Pennsy had building and repair shops at Altoona, Pennsylvania as well as in other major cities it served, but it was the Altoona shops that became famous for constructing locomotives, cars, iron bridges and rolling stock.

The Pennsy contributed a number of 'firsts' to the industry—the first railroad to set up a locomotive testing plant, the first to standardize locomotive drivers with cast-iron centers and wrought-iron tires (replacing chilled-tread cast-iron drivers), and the first to standardize its fleet of locomotives (in 1862) to increase economy and efficiency of operations.

The Pennsy was also the first major American railroad to switch from wood to coal driven steam locomotives when in 1853 it used Pennsylvania anthracite coal in a test. Within nine years, all PRR engines were coal burners and continued in use for 100 years. This was during a period when other railroads came to rely extensively on oil to fuel steam locomotives.

The Pennsy was long famous for its *Broadway Limited* high-speed passenger service which operated between Chicago and New York. *The Limited* competed head-to-head against NYC's *Twentieth Century Limited* and competed vigorously against its rival NYC right up until the fatal merger in 1970. Long before—in 1910—the Pennsy had gone so far as to tunnel under the Hudson River so that it could serve New York

City directly from its famed Pennsylvania Station in direct competition to the Central.

Beginnings

The Pennsy began in 1846 when it was granted a charter to offer service between Harrisburg and Altoona. After opening in 1850, the Pennsy quickly expanded service into other cities in Pennsylvania and acquired other railroads, among these some of the oldest in the United States, including the Camden & Amboy, the Philadelphia & Columbia, the Philadelphia, and the Germantown & Norristown.

To the Camden & Amboy went the honor of operating the first steam locomotive in the nation, *The John Bull*, constructed in 1831 at the Stephenson works at Newcastle-upon-Tyne, England. Interestingly, when the engine first arrived by ship, still disassembled, none of the employees knew how to

The Camden & Amboy's *John Bull (above)* **currently resides at the Smithsonian Institution.** *Below:* **Pennsy loco Number 212 was the Baldwin Work's 1000th in production.** *Above right:* **Pennsy electric locomotives, coupled back to back for a double header. Note the famous Pennsy four-track roadbed.**

assemble it. It was left to John Dripps, an apprentice mechanic, to reconstruct the engine, and the 10-ton, four-wheeled vehicle went into service in 1833.

It was also Dripps who suggested the addition of two pilot wheels to guide the engine around the many curves of the Camden & Amboy. Dripps made still other modifications, such as adding a fully enclosed fuel car (which gave it the appearance of a rolling shack). He also added bells, whistles and lights. Dripps was also responsible for the invention of the 'cowcatcher'—a familiar part of American locomotives during the steam era—which he first attached to the *John Bull*. The locomotive continued to be used until 1893, when it was retired and put on display at the Smithsonian Institution in Washington, DC.

Between 1830 and 1835, Pennsylvania experienced an explosion of railroad construction, soon possessing more trackage than any other state. For example, the PRR—by constructing new track and by purchasing and leasing existing state-owned lines—established connections between Philadelphia and Pittsburgh, making it possible to travel on *The Pioneer*, called the 'Fast Line,' between these two cities in three and one-half days in 1837.

Pennsy's predecessors offered a mishmash of track and railroad construction. Engineers for the Columbia Railroad, which ran from Philadelphia to the Susquehanna River, came up with many different track systems. Columbia's road was a double track, 81.6 miles in length, with track mileage totaling 163.2 miles. For the first six miles, the rails consisted of granite sills planted with flat iron bars. Sixteen miles had rails consisting of wooden string-pieces planted with thin iron bars laid on wood crossties. Two miles of the track of iron rails were supported by stone blocks, which kept the rails from spreading apart under the weight of the trains. Iron rails resting upon stone blocks with wooden cross-sills were used on the rest of the route.

Railroads found this construction needlessly expensive and soon adopted the materials now widely used, with rails attached to wooden crossties secured with gravel ballast. Iron was substituted for wood as early at 1850, and steel was used in place of iron after 1870 when rolled steel costs became low enough to permit its use in the manufacture of rails. The weight of the the rails increased from 50 to 85 pounds, then to 110 pounds to the yard. The use of heavier rail became necessary due to the increasing weight of engines and cars and the increase in speed of passenger trains and freight traffic.

Passenger Service

Passenger traffic as well as freight loadings were critical to the success of the Pennsy throughout the 19th century. By 1884, five trunk lines ran between New York and Chicago, with two under construction to serve its exploding passenger service. The Pennsy also developed suburban service to increase its passenger revenue. For instance, it constructed a line from Philadelphia to Paoli, 25 miles away, and then operated trains all day to encourage commuter traffic. It bought land in and around Paoli, subdivided it and sold it off to middle-class families looking for comfortable homes away from the city.

The Pennsylvania Railroad did not grow and prosper in the 19th century without major problems. In 1877, the Pennsy, along with other railroads, cut wages 10 percent to preserve its profit margin and doubled the length of its trains to eliminate train crews. The employees were furious, and staged the world's first major railroad strike. Pennsy employees joined those from other railroads to shut down the nation's rail system, and they almost succeeded.

In Pittsburgh, US troops were ordered in to restore order, but not before rampaging mobs had burned the rail yard and destroyed more than 100 locomotives and 500 boxcars. Disorder also occurred in other cities, such as Altoona, Easton, Bethlehem, Buffalo and in Chicago, where crowds stormed the terminal, and Omaha, where striking men wrecked locomotives and freight cars. Order was finally restored with federal troops, but not before the employees had established strong railroad unions.

During and after the Panic of 1873, the Pennsy prospered at a time when other lines were sinking into bankruptcy. One

Above: Five big steam locos bear the Pennsy logo in a photo symbolic of the Pennsy's glory days, when the line was the heart of the American railroad system. *Below left:* Legendary Pennsylvania Station in New York City. *Above opposite:* An engraving of the interior of the first Pullman sleeper.

reason was the fact that it had formed close alliances with the powerful men of the time, like John D Rockefeller and Andrew Carnegie, who brought the Pennsy considerable business in return for favorable rates.

At the turn of the century, the Pennsy's president, A J Cassatt, purchased a controlling interest in the Long Island Rail Road. He then joined with the NYC to purchase 45 percent of the Chesapeake & Ohio Railroad as well as the Norfolk & Western, the Reading and the Baltimore & Ohio. Eventually, the Pennsy bought controlling interests in these competing lines despite threats from Congress and the Interstate Commerce Commission to prevent it.

Cassatt started 20-hour service between New York and Chicago after the NYC began its famed high-speed *Twentieth-Century Limited* between the two cities. Cassatt decided to tunnel under the East River and open Pennsylvania Station in direct competition with the NYC to make his line more competitive.

In the first half of the 20th century, the Pennsylvania Railroad was in a constant state of expansion east of Pittsburgh. Tracks through cities were elevated, and new stations were constructed along major lines. West of New York, passengers rode over new steel tracks at Newark, Elizabeth, Rahway and New Brunswick.

Like many other railroads, the Pennsy came under government control during World War I and emerged after the war in far worse shape than before. But prosperity in the 1920s and the new opportunity to use electrified service to cut costs enabled the Pennsy to stay competitive against trucking companies, automobiles and its rival, the NYC.

The Pennsy electrified many of its main lines in the 1920s and 1930s, introducing the GGI shark-nosed electrified locomotives in 1934. Many of those same locomotives are still hauling Amtrack passengers 60 years later along the northeast corridor between Washington, DC and Boston.

Pennsy's widespread use of electric locomotives was motivated by the passage of an ordinance in New York City forbidding steam trains to run south of the Harlem River after 1908. The New York Central was the first railroad to electrify the tracks between its Grand Central Station and Groton, New York, and the Pennsy followed soon after. It later electrified its line between Washington and New York at a cost of $126 million, with trains running as fast as 60 miles per hour between Manhattan and Washington. It was the last major main line in the US to be electrified, and Amtrak continues to operate today along the heavily travelled corridor.

The Pennsy opened Pennsylvania Station (since demolished) to attract passenger traffic at a cost of $100 million, but it was a marvel of both size and convenience. Penn Station was constructed above what was essentially a tunnel railroad, which entered Manhattan under the East River and continued out of the city over the Hudson River to Long Island. For years, the Pennsy had brought passengers to Jersey City, then moved them by ferry to Manhattan. But with the opening of its East River tunnel, crews used electric locomotives to bring steam trains from New Jersey and Long Island directly into the station.

In the 12 years that ended in 1963, the PRR and the Central realized an average return on investment of 1.28 percent and 1.84 percent, respectively, far less than could be earned in government bonds or utility stocks. The merger was expected to create an economy of scale to ease operating costs in an era when the interstate highway system took an increasing amount of traffic away from freight trains.

Merger

When the Pennsy and the NYC merged on 1 February 1968, it became the largest transportation company in the United States, with assets valued as high as $7 billion—$4.5 billion of that invested in the actual railroads—the rest in real estate, pipelines, trucks, barges, water companies, coal mines, factories, hotels, amusement parks and warehouses. Yet it was unable to generate enough cash to meet its payroll.

Because both railroads were neglected in the 1930s and both operated round-the-clock during World War II, equipment and tracks had deteriorated rapidly, forcing both firms to double capital expenditures in order to upgrade equipment and trackage. But despite spending generously during the 1950s, the decline continued.

Added to the burden was the cost of operating the New York, New Haven & Hartford Railroad, which provided service throughout an extensive network in southern New England. The line declared bankruptcy in 1836, reorganized in 1947 and suffered a general decline in the 1950s and 1960s.

In the 12 years that ended in 1963, the PRR and the Central realized an average return on investment of 1.28 percent and 1.84 percent, respectively, far less than could be earned in

government bonds or utility stocks. The merger was expected to create an economy of scale to ease operating costs in an era when the interstate highway systemtook an increasing amount of traffic away from freight trains.

The Story of the Pullman

After Commodore Cornelius Vanderbilt gained control of the New York Central, he took an important role in the development of the sleeping car. First conceived in the early days of railroading, various sleeping arrangements aboard passenger trains were tried throughout the 1840s and 1850s. But it was Webster Wagner, a wagonmaker, who came up with a workable idea and sought out Vanderbilt's help to finance construction of four test cars.

Featuring a single tier of berths and bedding closets at each end of the car, they were put into use on the New York Central. Within a few months, customers were clamoring to get aboard. Wagner later organized his own company to build and operate sleeping cars.

Despite Wagner's early success, it was George Pullman who was eventually best known for his 'Palace Cars' or 'Boudoirs.' A native New Yorker, Pullman had learned something of the art of moving when he demonstrated how to move a brick building from the path of the Erie Canal. He then made his reputation—and small fortune—raising a brick building in Chicago with the aid of 1200 workers so that another story could be added. The workers used 5000 jack screws to lift the building, a feat highly publicized in the local papers.

Pullman then became interested in building a railroad sleeping car. The Chicago & Alton Railroad gave him two coach cars to convert—at his own expense—and he put sleeping sections together with a linen locker and washrooms. The upper berths could be folded up when not in use, a radical idea for the time. He provided no blankets or sheets, but he did install candle lights and wood stoves before the cars made their first run in September 1858 from Bloomingdale to Chicago.

Bolstered by his success, he relocated to Colorado to refine his concept, creating *The Pioneer*. It was a foot wider and one-half foot higher than most passenger cars then in service and rode on improved trucks reinforced by solid rubber blocks to smooth the ride. He added carpets and mirrors and installed upper berths resting on hinges so they could be folded up when not in use.

The Pioneer was used to transport President Lincoln's body from Washington to Springfield, Illinois after his assassination in April 1865. The passage of Lincoln's funeral train was one of the major events of the century, with hundreds of thousands of people turning out along the towns and cities between Washington and Springfield. The widespread exposure helped to popularize the concept of a sleeping car. Not long after the Lincoln train, General US Grant rode *The Pioneer* from Detroit to his home in Galena, Illinois.

Soon Pullman was building more cars, and within two years he had organized the Pullman Palace Car Company and was charging 50 cents more per night than his competitors. Later, Pullman designed a hotel car, half-sleeper and half-restaurant, as well as an all-dining car, and soon was operating dining cars on a number of lines, although few railroads could make money with them.

By the late 1870s, Pullman had become one of the foremost industrial names in North America and was the nation's largest car-building and car-repairing company. Most railroads used his equipment because of its excellent reputation for service and quality. Even the Pennsy, after trying to run its own sleeping and dining service, gave up and came to Pullman.

He not only provided the cars to the railroads, he also provided his own employees—who worked for the passengers, not the railroads. Pullman established a level of comfort that has not been matched even by the airlines. He was the first to

introduce fresh linen and bedding in his sleeping cars, but it took a great measure of marketing to get customers used to the idea of taking off their clothes for a night of rest. For instance, the message 'Please take off your boots before retiring' was printed on tickets and on signs hung in the sleeping cars.

The Pullman dedication to service continued right up until the last passenger train service was handed over to Amtrak in the 1970s. Pullman had given millions of Americans a level of comfort and service unmatched today even by the airline industry. The firm originally founded to staff and service sleeping and dining cars has now ceased to exist.

Above: George Pullman, who made American rail travel downright comfortable. *Below:* Conrail engines pull a piggyback in Pennsylvania.

The Conrail Routes

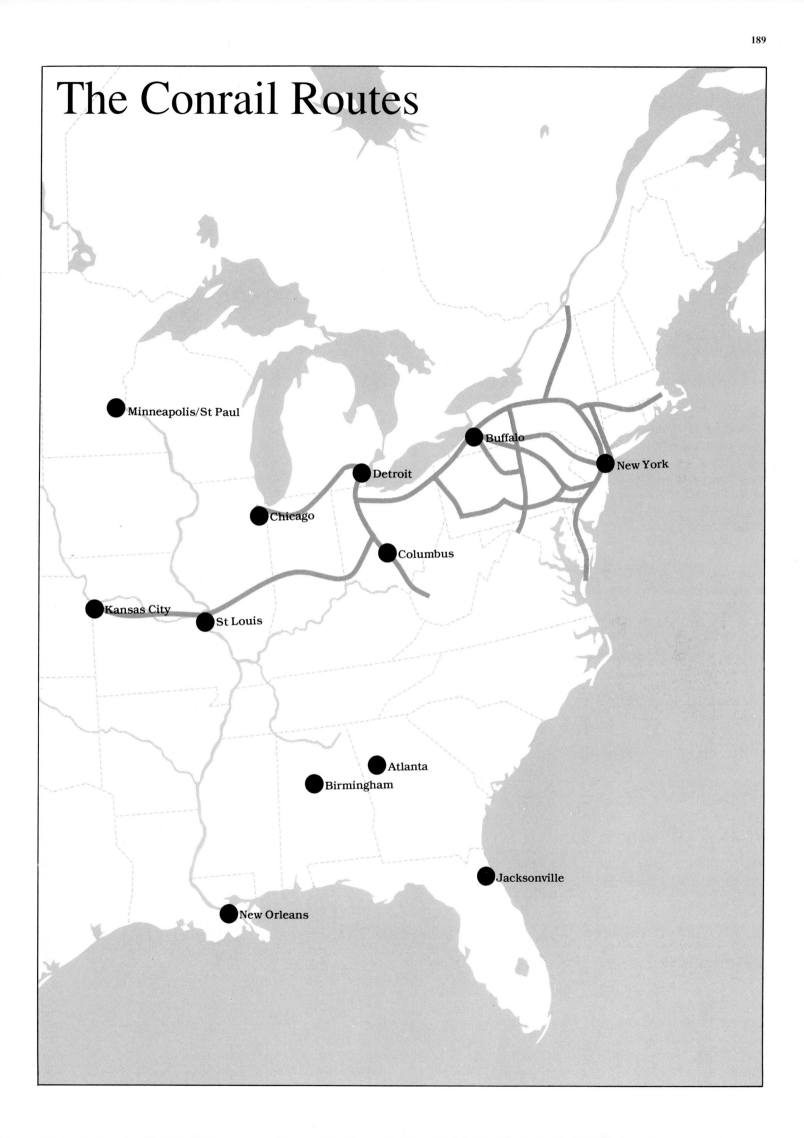

CONCLUSION

The history of these eight great North American railroads continues, but the romance of the rails has changed dramatically within the past two decades. Railroading is no longer a great adventure, but purely a commercial enterprise. Furthermore, in an age of mergers and acquisitions, many of the great names of railroading have changed or disappeared. Unlike earlier days, railroading no longer plays an overriding role in the continent's economy.

Who would recognize the famous old names of the New York Central or the Pennsylvania Rail Road that are hidden within the name of Conrail? Who would have dared to predict that one day the mighty Southern Pacific would merge with the Atchison, Topeka & Santa Fe?

Events in history move rapidly. It has been less than three decades since the railroads of the continent used steam locomotives on their main lines; yet within that time, the business of railroading has changed tremendously, not only in its conversion from steam to diesel, but in fundamental aspects of the business.

Railroads are no longer growth industries. Indeed, they are shrinking industries—like steel or aluminum or copper. Although freight trains continue to haul recently minted automobiles from the factory to the distribution yard, as well as carry containerized goods and products from shipyard to market, railroads have conceded their subordinate role: trucks and automobiles now claim dominance over them, and highways—not railroads—form the backbone of North America's transportation system.

Long-haul trucks now carry a major portion of the freight in this country, and the once mighty railroads—like the Southern Pacific, the Union Pacific, the Burlington Northern, CP Rail and the Santa Fe—are now subsidiaries of diversified, publicly held companies that engage in a wide range of business and industrial activities. Many railroads make much of their money with special unit trains carrying such basic resources as coal from the mines to the utilities.

The recently formed Santa Fe Southern Pacific, for example, is engaged in commercial and industrial real estate development and energy development. Railroading contributes only a portion of the annual revenues of these conglomerates. In many instances, the profit returned on investment in today's railroads is far less than that returned from investment in other industries.

The process began many decades ago when Congress decided to subsidize construction of the US interstate highway system as well as the expansion of airports to handle jet passengers and cargo planes.

It was inevitable, after the Depression and World War II when the very structure of the nation's economy changed, that railroads would no longer dominate the imaginations of the American people or dominate the political and social structure of American and Canada as they did in the 19th century.

So what lies ahead for railroading and for the continent's great railroads?

Many more mergers and acquisitions are expected in future years, along with a decline in the number of miles of tracks in service by US and Canadian railroads. Trackage has been shrinking since World War I, when railroading reached its peak, and all the signs indicate that this will continue in the years ahead as the industry adjusts from an industrial-based to a service-based economy.

Larger and more efficient locomotives will haul a greater number of specialized cars—like double-stack flat-bed units—to carry cargo containers from shipside to customer dock as efficiently and economically as possible.

Railroads will not disappear, but they will become leaner and more efficient. They will have to.

The fact that the great railroads prospered is a tribute to the men of early railroading. They had grand schemes and great vision and were willing to work to achieve their ambitions. Without them, railroading would not have brought the benefits of the industrial revolution to North America nor helped civilize the westward expanses of the continent.

Opposite: A Canadian Pacific freight enters the upper portal of a complex spiral tunnel system in rugged British Columbia. Engineering marvels such as this tunnel system—and indeed, every facet of today's rail systems—would not be possible without fellows like these *(below),* the men who build them.

Index